SPACE LAW

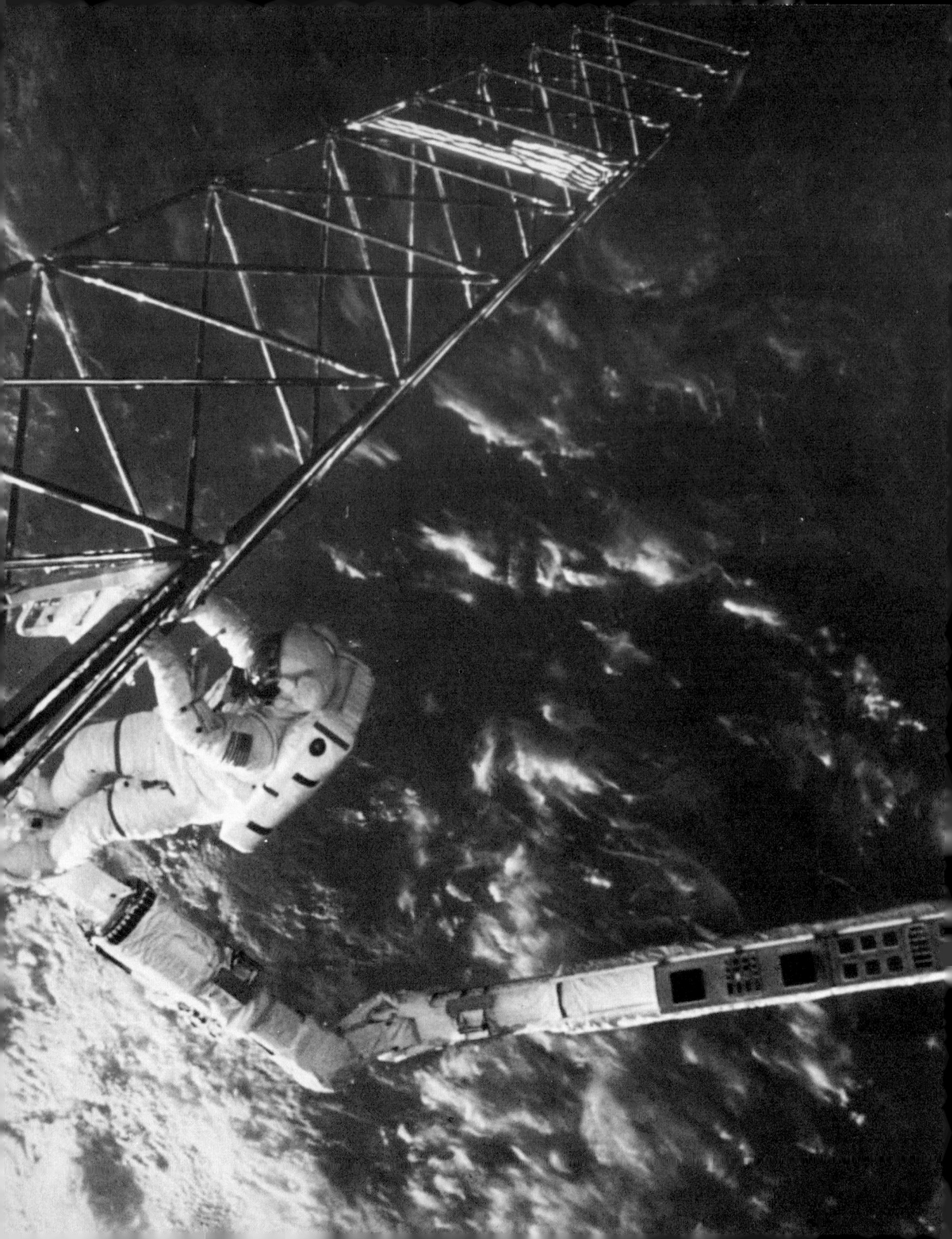

SPACE LAW

NECIA H. APFEL

Franklin Watts
New York ▪ London ▪ Toronto ▪ Sydney ▪ 1988
A First Book

Cover photograph courtesy of TRW, Inc.
Diagram by Vantage Art, Inc.
Photographs courtesy of:
NASA: pp. 2, 11, 20 (bottom), 24, 25, 27, 28, 30, 31, 46, 49, 51, 54 (top left), 59, 64 (top), 66, 80, 82, 85; Trustees of the Science Museum: p. 10; The Bettmann Archive, Inc.: p. 12; Air Force Photo: p. 14 (bottom); Library of Congress: p. 14 (top); United Nations: p. 16; Necia Apfel: p. 19; Jet Propulsion Laboratory: p. 20 (top); Yerkes Observatory: p. 23; Tom Kelly: p. 34; Virginia Museum of Fine Arts: p. 36; UPI/Bettmann Newsphotos: p. 38; Boeing Aerospace Company: p. 41; Bell Labs: p. 25 (top right), 54 (top right); Hughes Aircraft Company: pp. 54 (bottom), 55, 64 (bottom); Northwestern University/Herb Comess: p. 62; Los Alamos National Laboratory: p. 72; Department of Defense: pp. 75, 77.

Library of Congress Cataloging-in-Publication Data

Apfel, Necia H.
  Space law / by Necia H. Apfel.
     p.   cm. — (A First book)
  Bibliography: p.
  Includes index.
  Summary: Discusses the complex legal issues involved in modern space travel and exploration that have become the basis for much international debate since the space age began in 1957 with the launch of Sputnik.
  ISBN 0-531-10599-7
  1. Space law—Juvenile literature. [1. Space law. 2. Law.]
  I. Title II. Series.
JX5810.A64   1988   88-10259   CIP   AC

Copyright © 1988 by Necia H. Apfel
All rights reserved
Printed in the United States of America
5 4 3 2 1

CONTENTS

Chapter One
Introduction
9

Chapter Two
Our Place in Space
18

Chapter Three
What Are Laws?
33

Chapter Four
Control of Outer Space
45

Chapter Five
A Question of Soveriegnty
58

Chapter Six
Star Wars and the Law
71

Chapter Seven
Space Colony Law
79

Sources Used 88

Index 91

SPACE LAW

CHAPTER ONE

INTRODUCTION

On October 4, 1957, the Soviet Union launched the first artificial satellite, *Sputnik 1.* The world was stunned. The Space Age had begun.

Sputnik 1, by present standards, was very small, weighing only 184 pounds (83 kg). Today's spacecraft are thousands of tons, and even bigger ones are being planned. But the Soviet craft was the first to orbit the earth, an accomplishment long dreamed about by many people.

However, this was not the first time that rockets had been used to propel objects skyward. The history of rocketry can be traced back to the ancient Chinese, who invented both rockets and the black powder that was originally used to propel the missiles. We now call this black substance "gunpowder." Its use in rockets has long since been replaced by more reliable and less dangerous compounds.

With *Sputnik 1* and subsequent satellite launchings by both the United States and the Soviet Union during those early days of the Space Age came concern over many legal issues—issues

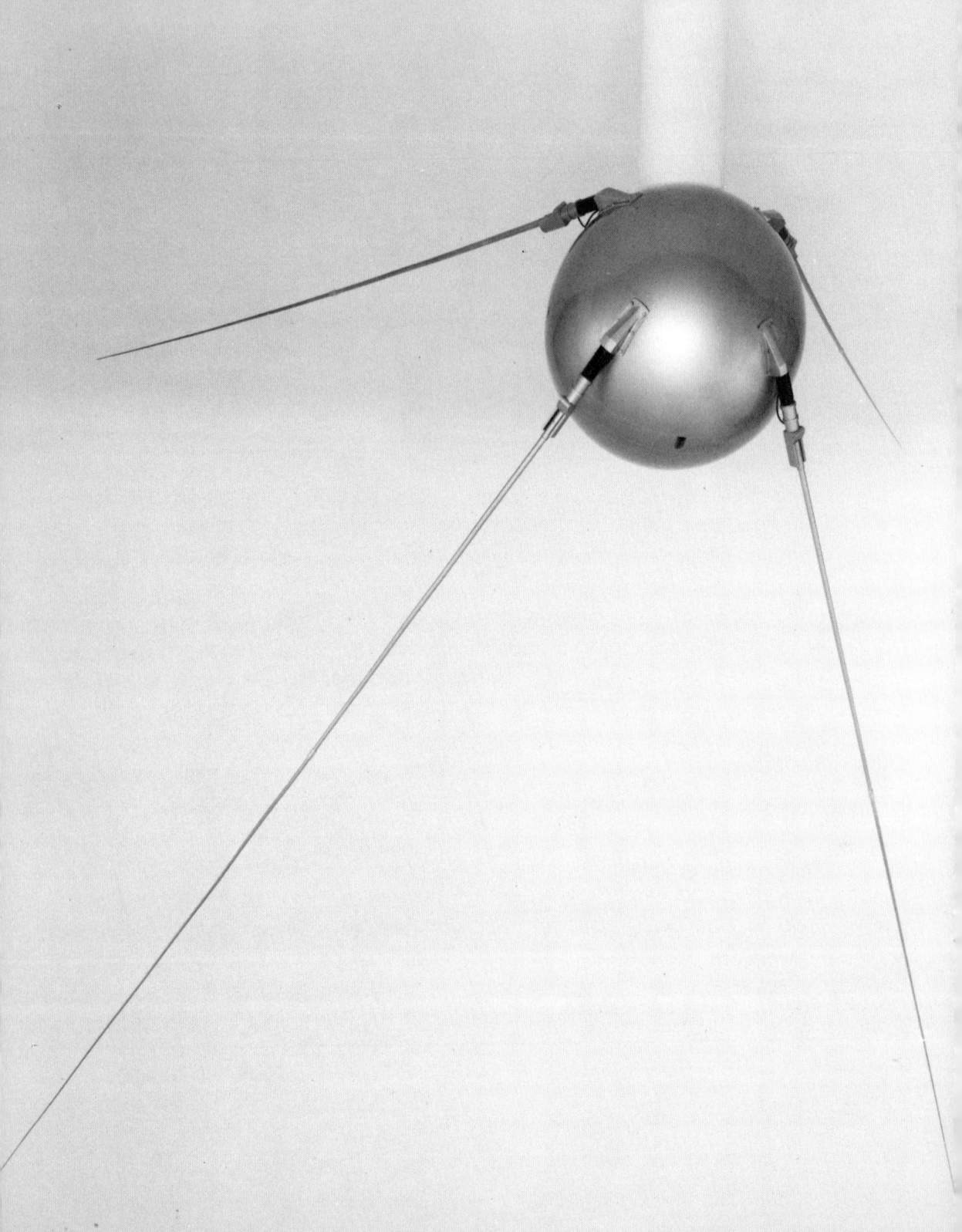

Left: *model of* Sputnik. Above: *an early launch of a Delta rocket to put a weather satellite into geostationary orbit.*

ancient Roman law court, with a woman pleading before a stern judge

that, in many cases, had not even been considered previously. A new field of law was opened up, and it has been expanding rapidly ever since. Legal writings concerning outer space have become voluminous. The number of words on the subject possibly exceeds even what engineers and scientists have written about the technical aspects of space.

The origins of space law, however, go back much further than the 1950s. Most of it comes from the field of aviation law, which itself only developed in recent times, that is, in the twentieth century. Behind both are the principles of common law, dating back to ancient Rome.

During the time of the Roman Empire, more than two thousand years ago, the air we breathe was judged to be in the same category as the water in the oceans. Unlike the land, which could easily be divided into individual properties, the atmosphere, like the oceans, was considered too vast to be owned or controlled by any one person or government. Instead, the oceans and air were open to the free use of all people.

Of course, even the Romans recognized that landowners owned the airspace directly over their own property if it was being used for some purpose. This allowed houses, fences, and other structures to be built upon the land. And it allowed owners the right to prohibit others from trespassing upon their land. But the space above the tallest buildings or trees belonged to everyone equally. No one could appropriate it for his or her own use. However, until the twentieth century, no one other than some balloonists, glider plane pilots, and kite fliers had much use for such space, and, therefore, it never became a controversial issue.

Not until flying really got under way in the early twentieth century was the idea of airspace as common property challenged.

National governments insisted that they be able to control what went on above and around their territories, particularly in regard to airplanes, in the same way that they were able to control activities upon their land and surrounding waterways. International conventions were held as early as 1889. At a 1919 convention, national representatives quickly agreed that the earlier "freedom of the air" concept was outdated. Now that air travel was becoming more commonplace, regulation was deemed necessary. The sovereign right of every nation to regulate the airspace above its own territory was recognized and has since become an integral part of international law.

Today we take this situation for granted. We know that one country can bar another country's planes from entering its airspace just as it can stop a foreign country's ships from entering its territorial waters or its land. In fact, entering the land, sea, or airspace of a foreign country without permission can be considered an act of war. As an example, because the United States and Cuba do not have diplomatic relations with each other, American planes are not allowed to fly over Cuba on their way to other Caribbean islands or to South America, even though it means they must go out of their way to get there.

On the other hand, allowing countries to regulate their own airspace activities has encouraged the development of the avia-

Charles Lindbergh (inset), an early pioneer in aviation, is shown here flying with an escort from Panama to Colombia in 1928.

a busy runway at a modern airport

tion industry in many countries. By governments granting air routes, developing airports, supporting research and subsidizing airlines with mail routes, and giving aircraft companies military contracts, a huge private industry has emerged. Starting an airline was a risky business venture in the early days of aviation. Safety regulations and control of the airspace had to be established before private enterprise would gamble on a form of transportation that many believed would never compete with railroads and ocean liners.

Today, the situation regarding outer space is similar to that of aviation in those early days of development. Laws are being formulated that, it is hoped, will encourage private enterprise to invest in outer space activities and at the same time will control these activities, both private and governmental. However, technological progress has been far more rapid than the development of effective laws to govern the space beyond the earth.

To understand this situation, we must first have some knowledge of the space that is being discussed. We must know what outer space is and how the earth relates to it. Then we can discuss the role of law in outer space.

CHAPTER TWO

OUR PLACE IN SPACE

We earthlings are the inhabitants of a small planet, the third one from a star that we call the sun. Our planet, the earth, is about four and a half billion years old and, in the words of modern technology, is a self-contained, recycling, solar-powered, life-support system. It is the only planet of this type that we know about in the entire universe. Each year the earth, with us aboard, travels half a trillion miles in its orbit around the sun. And the sun, with its family of nine planets, including the earth, travels 8 trillion miles through our galaxy, the Milky Way. No wonder many have called our planet "Spaceship Earth."

Of the eight other planets orbiting the sun, four are many times larger and more massive than our planet. These giant planets—Jupiter, Saturn, Uranus, and Neptune—are five to thirty times farther away from our sun than we are. Closer to us and to the sun are Mercury, Venus, and Mars, but even these planets are very far away from us compared with any distances here on earth. And tiny Pluto, the farthest planet, is about thirty-eight times farther away from us than the sun, which is 93 million miles away!

earthrise over the moon

Therefore, we usually think of our solar system as a very large place. We know that it takes many months or even years for our spacecraft to travel to any of the planets. However, if the universe were somehow suddenly shrunken in size so that Pluto was only about a yard (1 m) away from the earth, the next nearest star to our sun would still be 4.33 miles (6.9 km) away. The brightest star that we can see in the northern hemisphere, Sirius, the Dog Star, would be 8 miles (12.8 km) away. And the North Star would be well over 300 miles (480 km) away.

All of these stars, including the sun, are part of our galaxy, the Milky Way. There are probably several billion stars in the Milky Way, most of them much closer to its center than we are. In fact, our solar system is closer to the edge of our galaxy than it is to its center. Using the same scale as above, the Milky Way would shrink to about 100,000 miles (160,000 km) in diameter if Pluto were a yard (1 m) from the earth.

Of course, the Milky Way is not the only galaxy. There are billions of others. Many are much smaller, but some are enormously bigger. Some are so far away from us that they look like dim stars or faint smudges on photographs taken through the

Above: *Jupiter and its four largest moons, as seen by the* Voyager 2 *spacecraft during its historic flyby.* Below: *the landscape of Mars, as seen by the* Viking *spacecraft, which landed on the Martian surface.*

most powerful telescopes in the world. We are a very small part of the universe.

However, for us the earth is not small. Almost five billion people live upon its surface, and that number is increasing daily. One hundred years ago most people would have said that the earth was the only territory we could occupy. But our ideas have changed radically since then, because our technological advances have enabled us to travel beyond the earth. With the invention of the airplane, we were able to view the earth from above its surface. We also became able to move around our planet with greater speed, making our contacts with people and places all over the world more frequent.

In the last thirty years, we have moved even farther out, into outer space. Of course, with the exception of two satellites, *Pioneer 10* and *Voyager 1*, we have not reached beyond the solar system, but there is no doubt that the Space Age has begun. And with it has come a plethora of questions, problems, disputes, and conflicts. Not all of these have to do with science or engineering. Many arise from relationships between people, governments, industrial corporations, and the military. Somehow, if we are to move peacefully and economically into outer space, we must learn how to handle these situations.

Disputes that have already arisen and those that are bound to arise in the future must be mediated. The social problems that have already been foreseen by many sociologists and psychologists must be solved. And rules or laws that can be applied to this new frontier must be developed. Unlike the settling of the western United States, individuals are being sent into space by their governments. They are under governmental controls and as citizens must obey the laws of their countries. It would be practically

*the Andromeda Galaxy,
the galaxy nearest to our own*

the Pioneer *(left) and* Voyager *(above) spacecraft, both visitors to other worlds*

impossible for an astronaut to go into space on his or her own the way pirate ships sailed the oceans a few hundred years ago.

But outer space presents other problems. For example, where does the earth's atmosphere end and space begin? Although all countries recognize that the airspace above a nation belongs to that nation, there is controversy over how high up that airspace extends. And the controversy heats up when questions are raised about control and ownership of outer space and the objects that are there.

What happens if a piece of a spacecraft or satellite falls on another nation's land? This happened in January 1978, when debris from the Russian satellite *Cosmos 954* landed in northwest Canada after only four months in orbit. Satellites reenter our atmosphere frequently, but *Cosmos 954*, unlike most others, was powered by a nuclear reactor. Canada spent $14 million cleaning up the radioactive debris.

It wasn't until 1981 that the Soviet Union finally repaid $3 million of that amount. Canada might never have been reimbursed at all, however, if it had not been for international treaties that addressed such mishaps. And with more and more spacecraft and satellites circling the earth, there has been a call for even more detailed agreements and stricter controls, especially for nuclear-powered spacecraft. No one was injured or killed by *Cosmos 954*, but eventually such a tragedy could occur. Who would be responsible? Who would compensate the victims? Who would do the necessary cleanup work or repairs?

After the Chernobyl nuclear accident in 1986, two additional treaties were signed at a meeting in Vienna. Although the Chernobyl accident involved a nuclear power plant in the Soviet Union, these new treaties, along with the outer space treaties,

Successful launch of the space shuttle Challenger *in February 1984. In January 1986, the* Challenger *would be destroyed in a tragic explosion, killing its crew of seven.*

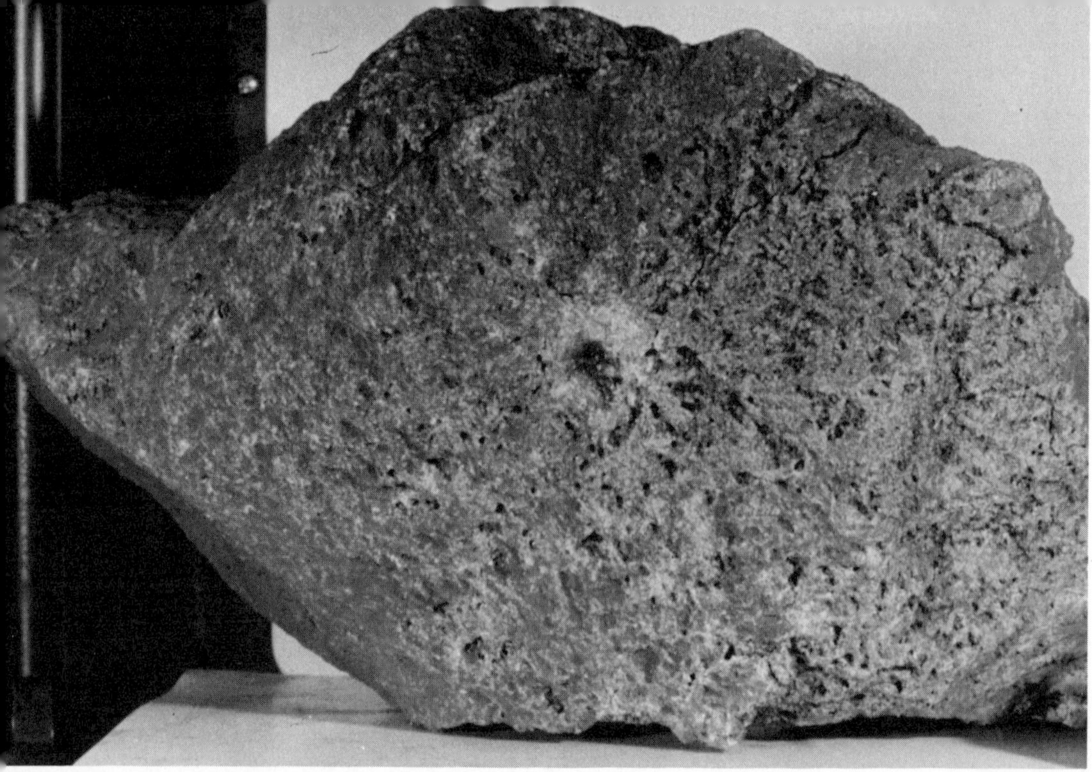

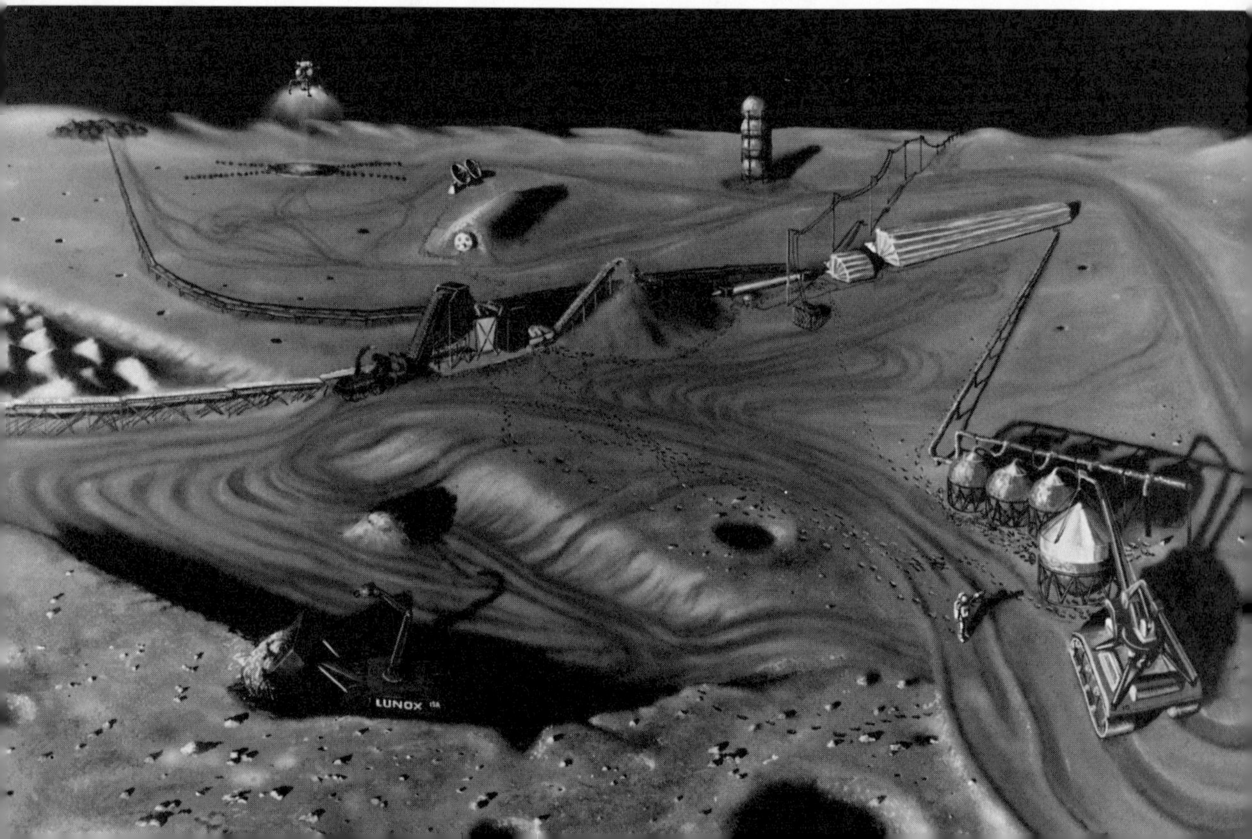
LUNOX

will help to answer some of these questions should they arise again.

Astronauts from the United States brought back rock samples from the moon during the Apollo mission in the early 1970s. No one questioned the ownership of these samples, but someday we may be able to mine much greater quantities of material from the moon, the asteroids, and Mars. Who will own such raw materials? Who, if anyone, will own the moon?

On a number of space shuttle trips, six or seven men and women lived for a week in outer space. Astronauts and cosmonauts stayed aboard the American *Skylab* and the Russian *Salyut* for periods ranging up to many months. In the future, longer trips are envisioned. If an astronaut commits a crime during such a mission, who is authorized to bring him or her to justice? What laws would govern such a situation? What if the astronaut is not an American citizen but is aboard an American spacecraft? Several foreigners have already participated in space shuttle flights and more will do so in the future. Multinational space crews may very well become the norm on a space station or in a space colony, and it is essential that there be adequate laws to protect and govern them.

Above: *a closeup view of the largest rock sample obtained during the* Apollo 15 *moon mission.* Below: *this artist's concept of lunar mining operations illustrates the production of liquid oxygen.*

Above: *the Skylab space station, home to a number of American astronauts in the 1970s.* Right: *the launching of an Indonesian communications satellite from the space shuttle's cargo bay*

Private industrial companies have been encouraged to place experiments aboard the shuttle and other spacecraft to see if better products can be made in space. Privately owned communications satellites have also been launched from the shuttle or by rockets. These ventures have been insured, but many insurance companies are hesitant to insure future ventures because of what is perceived as a greater-than-normal risk. Will insurance companies be able to charge high enough rates and still allow private space ventures to be profitable? Should the U.S. government help with this insurance, as it has done with nuclear power plants? Should our tax laws be adjusted to give these emerging industries help in getting established in space?

These are some of the questions that space lawyers are wrestling with. They are trying to solve these problems and, at the same time, anticipate future ones that are sure to arise. They must deal not only with the laws of their own countries but also with international law.

Unfortunately, as we will see, there are very few national or international laws that encompass outer space. In many instances, existing laws must be stretched or precedents from similar situations here on earth must be applied. Usually such treatment is inadequate, but at present there is no other alternative. The subject is very new and is completely different from any other area of law.

Before we look specifically at the existing treaties relating to outer space, let us consider laws in general. What are laws? What are international laws? What are treaties between nations?

CHAPTER THREE

WHAT ARE LAWS?

What are laws? They are the formalized rules of the society in which we live. Laws are made so that everyone knows what kind of behavior is expected from him or her and from everyone else. And, if you are caught disobeying these laws, the society in which you live will punish you.

A family is a small society; it has rules that members are expected to adhere to. Of course, these rules do not carry the same weight as the laws of our city, state, or country, but as with laws, disobedience of the rules may result in punishment.

Of course, not all families have the same rules. Even those living next to each other may have quite different rules of behavior. For example, you may be allowed to go out and play after school while another child must do homework or chores before playing. Perhaps your family requires that everyone finish eating before anyone leaves the dinner table; another family may allow the children to leave whenever they want to go.

Besides your family, you also belong to several larger societies. For example, your teacher, classmates, and you make up a

All games, including the favorite American pastime of baseball, have rules that must be followed to avoid chaos.

society that is different from your family group. Larger societies of which you are a member include your town, your state, and, of course, your country. Each of these has its own set of laws or rules that help determine how you live. For example, many communities have zoning laws that keep businesses out of residential areas. There are many traffic laws to regulate the movement of cars, trucks, and even bicycles. Your school may have rules regarding the clothes you wear to class each day or regulations controlling your right to be out of your classroom when school is in session.

Sometimes the rules or laws of one group or society conflict with those of another. If you are a member of both, you sometimes may not know what action to take in a particular situation. Or if two people from different groups are involved in the same activity, conflicting rules or laws may require a third party to settle disputes. You and your friends may play a game during recess using different rules than some other group of children. If you all play together, someone has to decide which rules will be followed. Otherwise the game will become chaotic.

To avoid chaos and conflict, people have always had rules to regulate behavior. Some were just customs, generally accepted by all but never codified into laws. Those that became laws were very carefully documented in constitutions and other legal papers. However, even with these laws, some were enacted because "that was the way it was always done." Others were voted on by the people themselves or their representatives. And still others were enforced by strong rulers who dictated how everyone would live and act.

Even the ancient tribes of wandering hunters had rules that governed their behavior toward each other and toward people

Washington addresses the Constitutional Convention in this painting by Junius Brutus Stearns.

from other tribes. Similarly, all nations today have laws for their own people and laws that govern their relationships with other nations. Laws that regulate the behavior between nations are called "international laws."

The basis for many of the laws in the United States today is the U.S. Constitution, although some laws are based upon English common-law principles that originated many centuries before the founding of the United States. Each individual state within the United States also has its own constitution, whose provisions are not allowed to conflict with those of the national Constitution. As with national laws, some state laws are based upon that state's constitution, whereas others have their roots in old English laws.

Most other countries also have some kind of constitution, although not all of these constitutions originated by democratic methods, as did the U.S. Constitution. However, there is no written constitution that regulates international law. The Charter of the United Nations established that organization, but it did not give the United Nations the power to control its members in the same way that a national government is able to control its citizens.

This weakness of the United Nations has created many problems. The situation was bad enough when the United Nations only had to deal with conflicts and disagreements occurring on the surface of the earth. But since October 4, 1957, when the Space Age began, the situation has become far more complex. Outer space is being looked upon not only as a territory for exploration and experimentation but also as an arena for possible conflict and hostilities.

Currently, many different types of artificial satellites are orbit-

the signing of the
Charter of the United Nations

ing the earth. Some are sending back useful weather information or are relaying messages and television shows to people all over the world. Others are being used as military "spy-in-the-sky" surveyors to obtain information about foreign activities. And there is also a tremendous amount of "space junk" orbiting the earth. This is debris left up there from earlier spacecraft.

We now know that humans can stay in space for long periods of time. We can walk and work on the moon and, no doubt, on other celestial bodies. The Soviet Union has already built and is orbiting a manned space station; the United States has plans to build and launch one by the end of the century. Many scientists believe that there will be people living in base camps on the moon and maybe even on Mars in the not-too-distant future. There are even plans to build a space colony sometime during the next century. It might house hundreds or even thousands of people. You may be one of those chosen to live in the colony. Or perhaps you will be one of the pioneers to journey to distant planets or even the stars. These ideas are no longer confined to science fiction. Some are becoming a reality.

There are, at present, only a limited number of international agreements or laws governing all these present and future space activities. The five original treaties that were ratified barely begin to address the serious problems that must be solved. And technological progress will not wait for international agreements to be given the necessary teeth of enforcement.

Before we consider the role of law in outer space, let us look at these five major space treaties.

1. **The 1967 Outer Space Treaty** (Treaty on Principles Governing the Activities of States in the Exploration and Use of Outer

Space, Including the Moon and Other Celestial Bodies). Signed January 27, 1967; ratified by eighty-five countries; date in force for the United States: October 10, 1967.

According to the 1967 Outer Space Treaty, the exploration and use of outer space is to be for peaceful purposes and to benefit all nations regardless of their economic or scientific development. This clause was not interpreted as requiring specific sharing of benefits but rather as a desire that space activities be generally beneficial to all. It went on to proclaim that outer space ". . . shall be the province of all mankind." Everyone was thereby assured equal access to outer space; no one could claim sovereignty over any part of it. The treaty also prohibited anyone from placing nuclear weapons or weapons of mass destruction into orbit around the earth, or stationing them in outer space or on any celestial body. Furthermore, each country signing the treaty agreed to give assistance to any astronauts in trouble and to assume liability for any harm resulting from its own space activities.

2. **Return and Rescue Agreement** (Agreement on the Rescue of Astronauts, the Return of Astronauts, and the Return of Objects Launched into Outer Space). Signed April 22, 1968; ratified by seventy-eight countries; date in force for the United States: December 3, 1968.

Elaborating on Article V of the 1967 Outer Space Treaty, this agreement required that endangered astronauts be given whatever assistance was possible and be returned safely and promptly to their own country if they were rescued by a foreign nation. Malfunctioning spacecraft were also supposed to be recovered, if possible, and, if requested, returned to whoever launched

This artist's drawing depicts the modules and other support systems of a possible orbiting space station designed by Boeing Company. On the right, extending from a remote arm, is an orbital maneuvering vehicle (OMV) and on the left are living, manufacturing, and laboratory modules.

them. This treaty did not define the term "astronaut" but referred to the "personnel of a spacecraft."

3. **Liability for Damages Convention** (Convention on International Liability for Damage Caused by Space Objects). Signed March 29, 1972; ratified by sixty-nine countries; date in force for the United States: October 9, 1973.

Space law is one of the very few areas of international law that has a specific agreement regarding liability. As its name implies, this convention stated that the country launching or authorizing the launch of a spacecraft is liable for any damage that craft does to people or objects on the ground or in the air. If the craft is already in orbit or in outer space, liability is based upon who caused the damage. The "launching state," moreover, is defined as not only the nation that actually launches the craft but also the one from whose territory the launch takes place. In cases where more than one nation participates in a space venture, liability is placed upon all the national participants and on any intergovernmental agencies involved in the launch and in the space activities.

The liability convention also provided for the establishment of a commission that would define the principles to be used in compensation claims. Note that liability is placed on national governments and not on individuals or private corporations. Each nation must therefore enact its own liability laws for private enterprises and for individual citizens. Thus, any harm that a U.S. spacecraft does to a U.S. citizen is covered by domestic law and not the liability convention. And to protect our government against any international liability claims, all commercial users of NASA launch facilities must have adequate liability insurance.

4. **Registration Convention** (Convention on Registration of Objects Launched into Outer Space). Signed January 14, 1975; ratified by thirty-four countries; date in force for the United States: September 15, 1976.

This convention required nations to register all space launches and to inform the UN secretary-general about the date and location of each launch, the orbital path of the spacecraft, and its general function once in space. Notification must also be given once the spacecraft is no longer in orbit. This agreement is important because it establishes a method of determining which nation has control and jurisdiction over a spacecraft as well as who is liable if a craft causes any damage.

5. **Moon Treaty** (Agreement Governing the Activities of States on the Moon and Other Celestial Bodies). Adopted by the General Assembly of the United Nations December 5, 1979; ratified by five countries (Austria, Chile, the Netherlands, the Philippines, and Uruguay), thus officially bringing it into force July 11, 1984; six other countries have signed but have not yet ratified the treaty (France, Guatemala, India, Morocco, Peru, and Rumania); neither the United States nor the Soviet Union has signed.

Repeating the 1967 Outer Space Treaty, the Moon Treaty required that the moon and other celestial bodies be used only for peaceful purposes, and prohibited placing any nuclear or mass-destruction weapons on these celestial bodies. The moon and its resources, it said, are the "common heritage of mankind" and cannot be appropriated or claimed for ownership by any one nation, organization, or individual. The resources, however, can be removed from the moon or other celestial bodies, but until such removal takes place, no one can claim ownership of such materials. The treaty also calls for the establishment of a future international agency that would manage the lunar resources and oversee their equitable distribution, with special consideration being given to developing countries.

These are the five major international treaties relating to outer space. Let us look more closely at the role these agreements have played in international relations and in activities in outer space.

CHAPTER FOUR

CONTROL OF OUTER SPACE

Why do we want to go out into space? It certainly isn't a hospitable environment. There is no air to breathe, no water to drink. There is no heat if the sun's rays are cut off. And yet exposure to the intense solar radiation can be lethal. Also, unless you are on the moon or another celestial body, you must contend with weightless conditions. At times that can be great fun, but it also can be treacherous if your spacecraft malfunctions. Even on the moon, gravity is much less than that of earth's. And on an asteroid it would be minuscule.

But the risks of entering outer space are more than offset by the advantages. First of all, there is the great thrill any adventurer receives from exploring new terrain. There will always be men and women willing to risk life and limb to climb the highest mountain, explore the deepest ocean, or soar into the hostile regions beyond the earth. Just as Columbus, Magellan, and others sailed unknown oceans five hundred years ago, so today astronauts are sailing the oceans of space.

But in addition to the adventurers and explorers are those

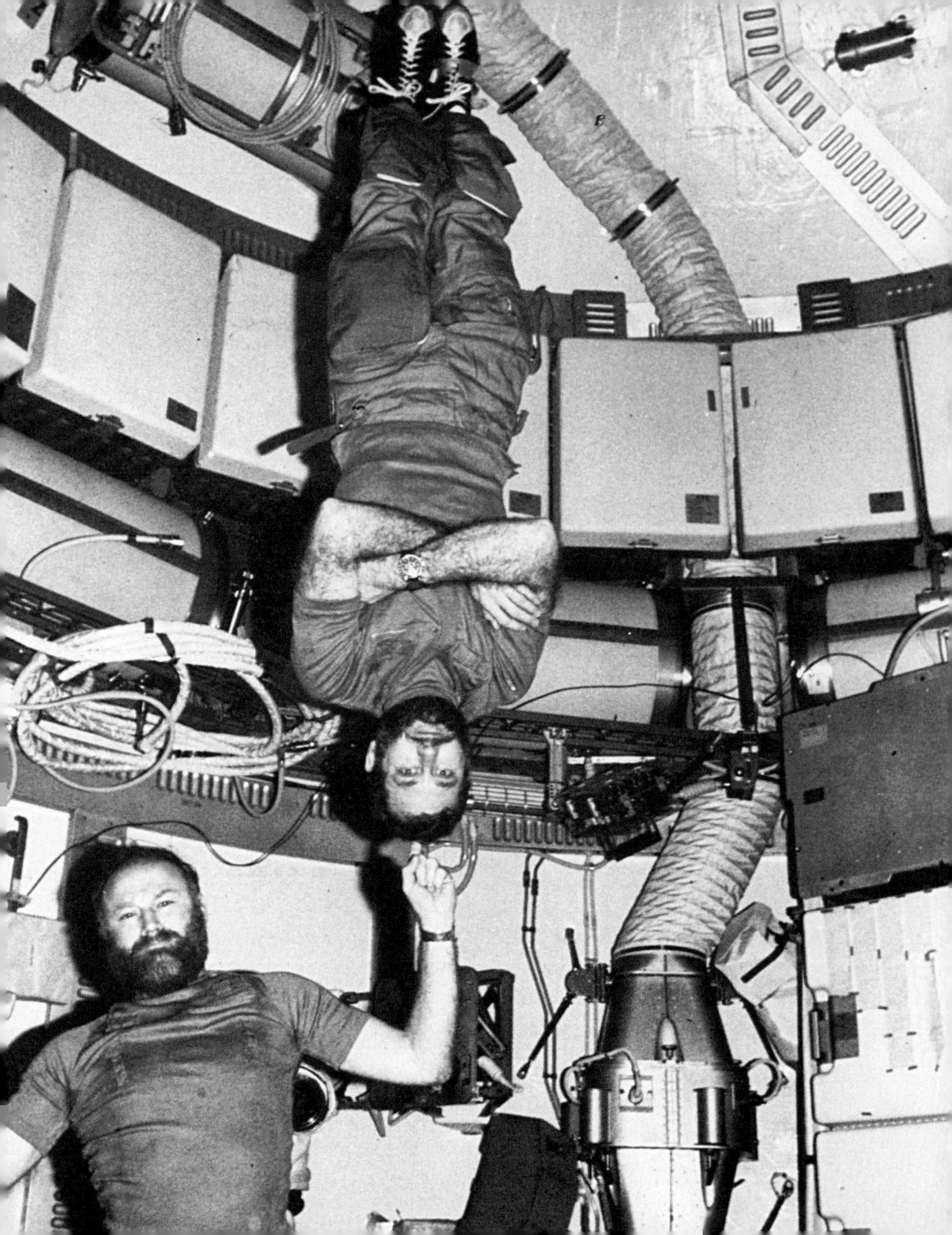

who seek to find practical uses for this newfound region. Better communications, advanced medicines, improved manufacturing processes, and more accurate weather forecasting are only some of the areas that have or will profit from space technology and exploration. And then there are the real pioneers, the counterparts of those who settled the American West. Men, women, and children of the twenty-first and twenty-second centuries may very well be able to live in space colonies or in settlements on the moon or other celestial bodies. There are many today who are already willing and eager to live in such places.

As we have seen, wherever men and women live, work, and relax together, they have established rules of behavior or laws. And outer space is no exception to this. As early as 1957, shortly after the first space probe, international space law began to be formulated, mainly by the United Nations. Since then, five major space law agreements and treaties have been hammered out. These were the ones summarized in the previous chapter. Note that with each succeeding treaty, fewer and fewer countries have signed it. The first treaty was agreed to by eighty-five countries, whereas the last one only by five. The United States and Soviet Union, for example, have never agreed to the last treaty, although both signed and ratified the other four.

The lack of gravity in space can be fun. It can also create serious problems for those living for long periods of time in space. Shown here are astronauts aboard Skylab.

Most of the provisions in these documents are noncontroversial, especially since the language used in many cases is quite vague and noncommittal. Declaring that outer space is to be "the province of all mankind" sounds marvelous but is open to all kinds of interpretations. Until more specific wording is presented, the phrase is unclear as to its legal meaning.

The controversy involving these international agreements really started with the Moon Treaty, in which the principle of "common heritage of mankind" was not only stated but also given a specific interpretation by the UN committee that wrote it. By the 1970s outer space was no longer thought of as being just the realm of science fiction writers and rocket enthusiasts. It held the future of much of the world's development and its control and utilization had become very important. Thus, the committee indicated that "common heritage of mankind" meant that there had to be an equitable sharing by all countries of all the benefits derived from lunar and other celestial body resources. And they added that the interests and needs of developing countries were to be given special consideration, even if those countries had not contributed to space exploration or development.

Like a similarly worded convention of 1982 pertaining to the world's oceans, this provision has given rise to much disagreement among nations, especially between the more technologically advanced and the less developed nations. It is one of the major reasons why so few countries have ratified the Moon Treaty. Governments and private business enterprises will be very hesitant to invest in lunar development if their profits are to be partially distributed to noninvestors. However, since it will be many years before any exploitation of lunar resources becomes a reality, there is still time to resolve this controversy.

The planting of the American flag on the moon was not meant to confer American ownership.

All of the outer space treaties declared that outer space, including the moon and other celestial bodies, cannot be owned by anyone. However, individual spacecraft still remain the property of the party or parties that launched them. This is true whether the craft is actually in space or has landed upon a celestial body. No one questioned the ownership of the *Apollo* spacecraft when it was in space or sitting on the lunar surface. And the placing of an American flag upon the surface of the moon did not confer American ownership, nor was it meant to do so.

However, space lawyers have already pointed out a legal dilemma here. If outer space belongs to everyone and cannot be appropriated by anyone, isn't a spacecraft that obviously occupies some of that space while in use appropriating that space while it is within it? Of course, up until now this situation has not caused any real legal problems. All spacecraft have been in space for only short periods of time, and compared to the immense volume of space, they are extremely small.

But there are already plans for much larger space structures, both in space and on celestial bodies. For example, NASA is studying the possibility of constructing large space colonies occupying over a million cubic meters of space. And both the United States and the Soviet Union are considering the deployment of large-scale strategic defense structures in space. Plans are also being made for the construction of lunar or planetary bases that could grow quite large. The potential for conflict exists if more than one nation wants to use the same regions of space or the same surface area on the moon or one of the planets.

One area of space that has already had conflicting claims is the "geostationary orbit." This is the corridor of space circling the earth that is most advantageous for communications satel-

This artist's drawing is of a Rockwell International "dual keel" space station design.

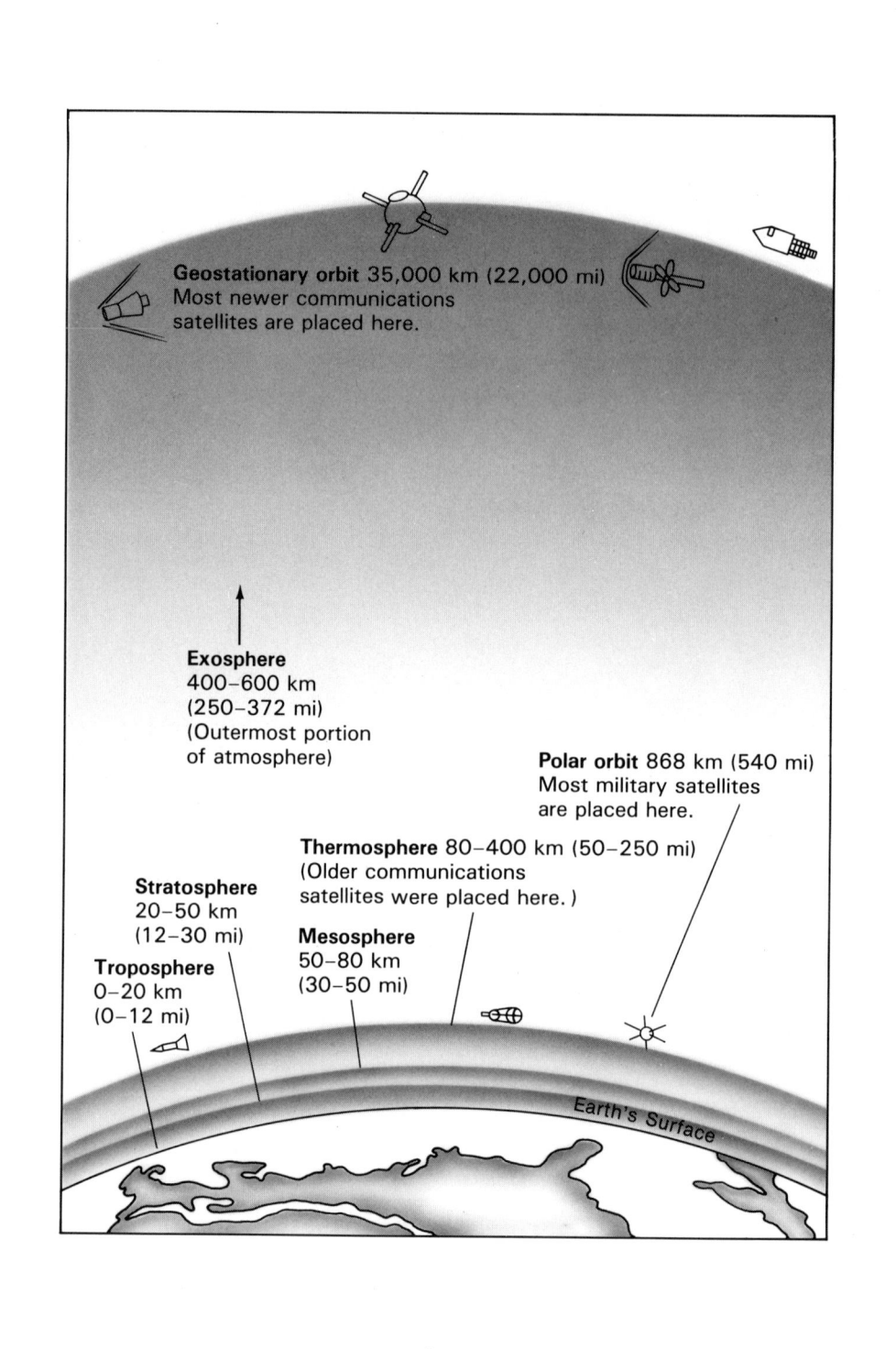

Geostationary orbit 35,000 km (22,000 mi)
Most newer communications satellites are placed here.

Exosphere
400–600 km
(250–372 mi)
(Outermost portion of atmosphere)

Polar orbit 868 km (540 mi)
Most military satellites are placed here.

Thermosphere 80–400 km (50–250 mi)
(Older communications satellites were placed here.)

Stratosphere
20–50 km
(12–30 mi)

Mesosphere
50–80 km
(30–50 mi)

Troposphere
0–20 km
(0–12 mi)

Earth's Surface

lites. A satellite in this orbit travels around the earth at the same speed and direction as the earth's rotation. By doing this, the satellite remains over basically the same spot on earth. It is necessary for the satellite to maintain a speed of 6,875 miles (11,000 km) per hour, 22,300 miles (35,680 km) above the equator, to achieve this effect.

A geostationary satellite can remain in constant contact with a specific surface area of the earth. Expensive tracking equipment is not needed to constantly reorient the ground receiver toward the satellite. Earlier communications satellites that were not in a geostationary orbit could send signals to the earth only when they came within range of ground stations.

Thus, the geostationary orbit has been called a natural resource, and in this age of instant communications, it is a very important one. However, despite its huge volume, it is not an unlimited natural resource. Geostationary satellites must be separated to prevent collisions or electrical interference with each other. The collision risk arises because each satellite does not stay in exactly the same position all the time. Due to natural forces from the earth, moon, and sun, the satellite is pulled in many directions as it orbits the earth.

When it drifts too far, small thruster jets mounted on the satellite move it back to within one-tenth of its desired position. But even with these corrections, the constantly drifting satellite must still have about 150 square kilometers (58 sq. miles) of space in which to move up, down, and sideways. The geostationary orbit is therefore not a thin line but rather a corridor of space 22,300 miles (35,680 km) above the earth's equator.

To avoid collisions between the drifting satellites, they can be placed in orbit as close as two-tenths of a degree apart. If that were the only consideration to their positioning, there would be

Top left: Echo, *the world's first communications satellite, made of Mylar and launched in 1958;* Top right: Telstar, *the first "active" communications satellite;* Left: *an artist's drawing of* Aussat, *a modern communications satellite serving Australia and launched in 1985.*

Small thruster jets, such as this one, are used to keep a satellite in its proper orbit.

enough room for some 1,800 of them in the geostationary orbit. But to prevent interference with each other's electronic signals, their separation must be far greater. Therefore, unless our technology improves greatly in this field in the near future, less than 450 satellites will be able to operate in this important orbit.

By 1985, over 126 such satellites had already been placed in the geostationary orbit. And because only certain regions of the orbit are useful for specific countries, some portions are relatively empty while others are very congested. The sections over the Pacific Ocean, for example, have very few satellites, whereas those encompassing the United States are almost filled.

Many nations are concerned that the best orbital positions within the geostationary orbit will be filled before they are ready to launch their own communications satellites. Some want to be able to reserve an orbit position for some future time, rather than maintaining the current "first come, first serve" policy that is currently followed by the International Telecommunication Union (ITU). The ITU is the UN agency that has been given the international responsibility for regulating the geostationary orbit satellites.

Even within the United States, however, because of the rapid development of a very competitive market, more equitable allocations had to be made regarding that portion of the geostationary orbit that services the United States. The Federal Communications Commission (FCC) in the United States assigns geostationary orbits for domestic use, and it has recently ruled that these positions are not permanent and that relocation at a later time is possible. Although this flexibility clause answers the changing needs of domestic satellite operators as well as the orbital needs of neighboring countries, the demand for domestic satellite service has far outstripped the capacity of the geostationary orbit section that can serve the United States. For this reason, the FCC is currently permitting closer spacing of satellites in the orbit above the United States.

The ITU originally assigned positions in the orbit based upon a country's needs and its ability to use the facility. But in 1982, this assignment method was replaced by one that took into account the special needs of developing countries and also the geographic location of a particular country. This change came about because of a 1976 declaration made by eight equatorial countries. Called the Bogota Declaration, it states that countries whose land lies on the earth's equator own the segments of the geostationary orbit over their own territories. The countries involved claimed the right to prior approval of any satellite placed in such a region of outer space and the right to govern the operation of that satellite.

The drafters of the Bogota Declaration—Brazil, Colombia, the Congo, Ecuador, Indonesia, Uganda, Kenya, and Zaire—argued that because the existence of the geostationary orbit depended upon the earth's gravity, it was physically linked to the earth and was not part of outer space. Most of the rest of the world rejected this argument even though a definition of where outer space begins has never been agreed upon. It was argued that because natural forces keep perturbing the motions of the satellites, they would drift off into space if their propulsion devices didn't keep them in the correct orbit. And it is the gravity of the entire planet, not the gravity within any one nation, that causes the geostationary orbit to exist. Therefore, no nation or group of nations can claim ownership of this region of outer space any more than it can claim other outer space regions.

However, to some extent, the Bogota Declaration has caused the ITU to change the way it allocates positions within the geostationary orbit. And this change poses a threat to the communications industry of the United States and other technically advanced nations who make heavy use of communications satellites. It is but one example of the way in which everyone is scrambling for the best foothold in the new terrain. There will undoubtedly be additional future claims to areas of outer space similar to the Bogota Declaration, and each will have to be dealt with separately, using the laws, conventions, and treaties that are current at that time. To understand some of these possible future conflicts, let us look at other potential areas of conflict in outer space.

CHAPTER FIVE

A QUESTION OF SOVEREIGNTY

The geostationary orbit hasn't been the only controversial area of outer space. Even the question of where outer space begins has plagued space lawyers ever since spacecraft entered this region.

How high does the earth's atmosphere extend? As we have seen, according to international law, airspace over a country's territory belongs to that country. And, according to all the outer space agreements and treaties, outer space—that is, the region beyond the atmosphere—belongs to all humankind. Therefore, many feel that it is imperative that some demarcation be drawn between the regions under national control and those belonging to everyone.

But the earth's atmosphere does not end abruptly. It gradually becomes thinner and thinner as we rise upward, until it becomes the extremely rarefied medium of outer space. But even in outer space a perfect vacuum does not exist. In the least dense regions of outer space we still find at least a few dozen protons, electrons, or other bits of subatomic matter within each golfball-

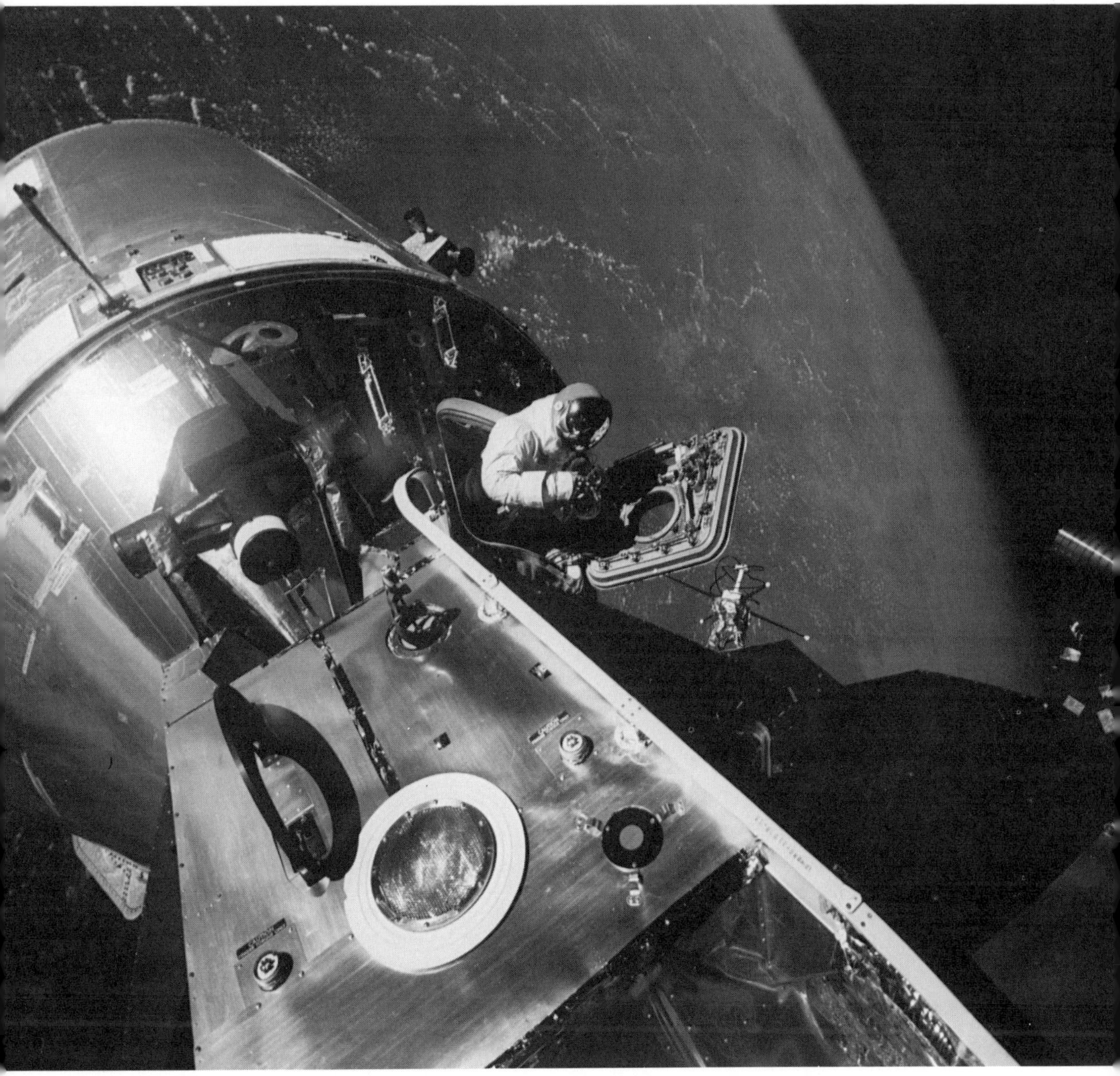

size volume of space. Of course, compared to the billions of atoms contained in a similar volume at sea level here on earth, that amount of material could never be classified as "atmosphere." But just where the earth's atmosphere ends cannot be precisely defined scientifically.

Because of this, there is still no international agreement about the boundary of outer space. The question was first raised in the United Nations as early as 1959. And it has been on and off the agenda of that organization ever since, with no solution in sight. However, three major points of view have surfaced in the many debates on the subject.

The first comes from those who would like to fix the boundary at a specific height, say 62 to 68 miles (100 to 110 km) above sea level. Those favoring this "spatial" point of view argue that since no natural line exists, any boundary agreed upon will be a legal and political one, not one based upon science or technology.

But it has been pointed out that it would be almost impossible for most nations to control such a high airspace, making the agreement largely ineffectual. These "functionalists" also believe that creating an artificial boundary may ultimately hinder technological developments in space. They argue that the activities and the vehicles used for these activities should determine if they are operating within the earth's atmosphere or in outer space. For example, some would place the boundary at the lowest point at which orbiting satellites can safely maintain their orbits. Since few satellites travel in perfectly circular orbits, there is a point at which the satellite is closest to the earth and another one where it is farthest away. The closest, or lowest, point is called its "perigee"; the most distant, or highest, point is its "apogee."

However, future craft may be able to achieve lower stable perigees than are now possible, thus changing the boundary line. There are also plans to attach a satellite by a long cable to the space shuttle and suspend it into the earth's atmosphere, to study layers of the upper atmosphere. How the functionalists will handle that kind of spacecraft in terms of its position and activity remains to be seen.

Because of all these uncertainties, the third view regarding the boundary of outer space is one of "wait and see." So far, regulations regarding space have proceeded satisfactorily without any precise definitions of where it begins. And until we know more about outer space and how we will use it, these proponents argue that there should be no attempt to rigidly define it.

Even as lawyers and diplomats wrestle with attempts to define outer space, how the information derived from satellites in outer space will be used has been hotly debated. Many satellites are programmed to survey the earth's resources, using telephoto and wide-angle cameras, infrared telemeters, spectrometers, and other sophisticated instruments. Some, orbiting at about 62 miles (100 km) above the earth's surface, are capable of seeing the numbers on a license plate or detecting the outlines of warm footprints on jungle trails.

These are "remote-sensing" satellites, which employ a technology that dates back to the nineteenth century, when observation balloons began carrying cameras to photograph the earth's surface. Later, airplanes and high-altitude balloons carried on this work. With the advent of the Space Age and the development of much more advanced sensing devices, remote sensing has become the most important tool in surveying and managing earth's natural resources.

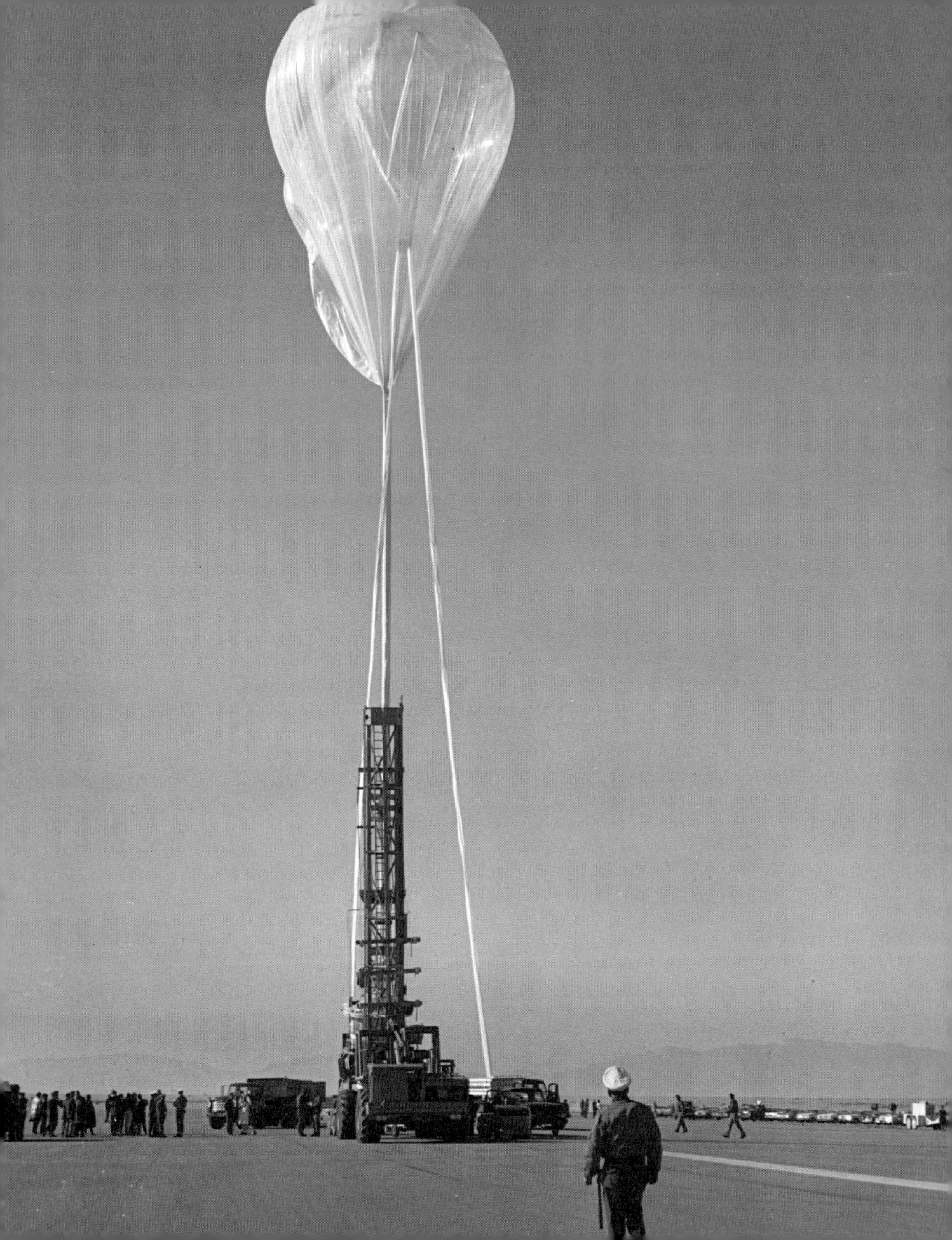

Remote sensing depends upon the electromagnetic radiation emitted by material objects. Every material object that has a temperature above absolute zero (−273° centigrade) radiates, or reflects, electromagnetic radiation. We are most familiar with this radiation in the form of light, but there is an entire spectrum of electromagnetic radiation from the very short waves of gamma rays and X rays through the visual spectrum to the long waves of radio and television. The wavelength of the radiation determines what form the radiation will take. Cooler objects emit electromagnetic radiation with longer wavelengths than do warmer ones.

With remote-sensing devices recording electromagnetic radiation, observation satellites have progressed greatly since the first one, a weather satellite, was launched in 1960. Today, there are many such satellites constantly sending information about weather conditions to ground stations around the world. They show where frontal systems are, give warnings about severe storms, and measure rainfall and atmospheric temperatures. Our weather forecasters rely heavily upon the data that these satellites supply.

During the U.S. Mercury and Gemini space programs in the 1960s, astronauts took the first land survey photographs from space with hand-held cameras. These and experiences from earlier weather satellites led the way by 1972 to a larger program in

a high-altitude balloon
for remote sensing
and weather forecasting

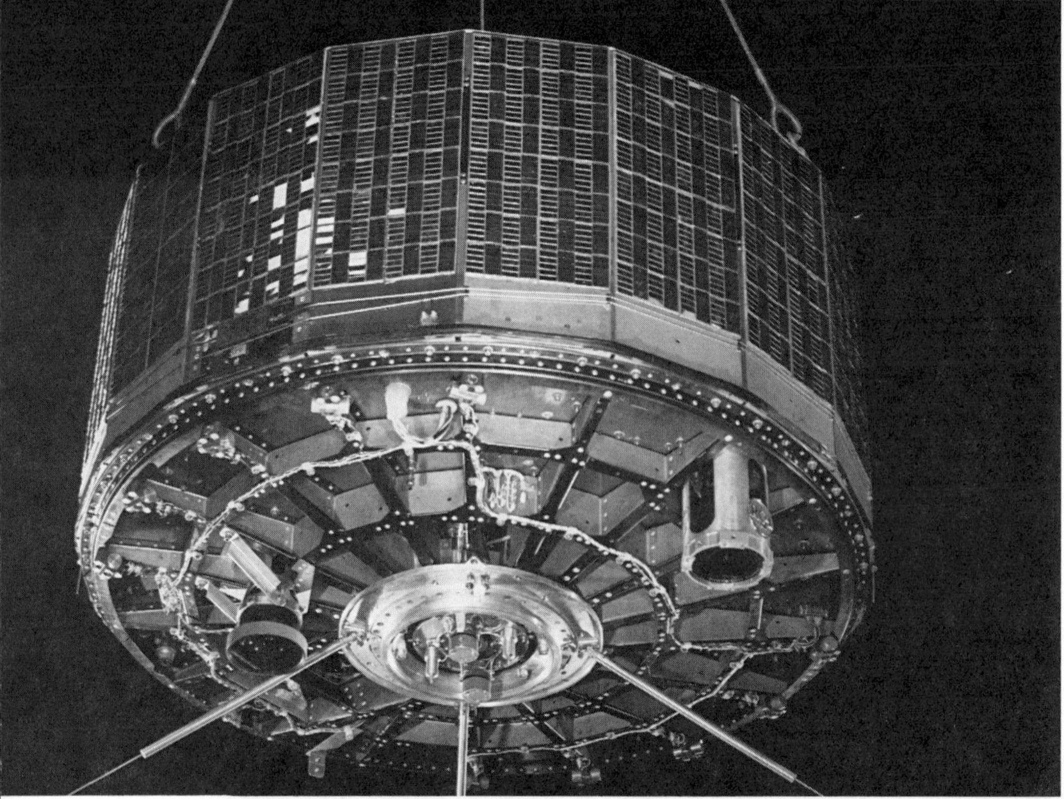

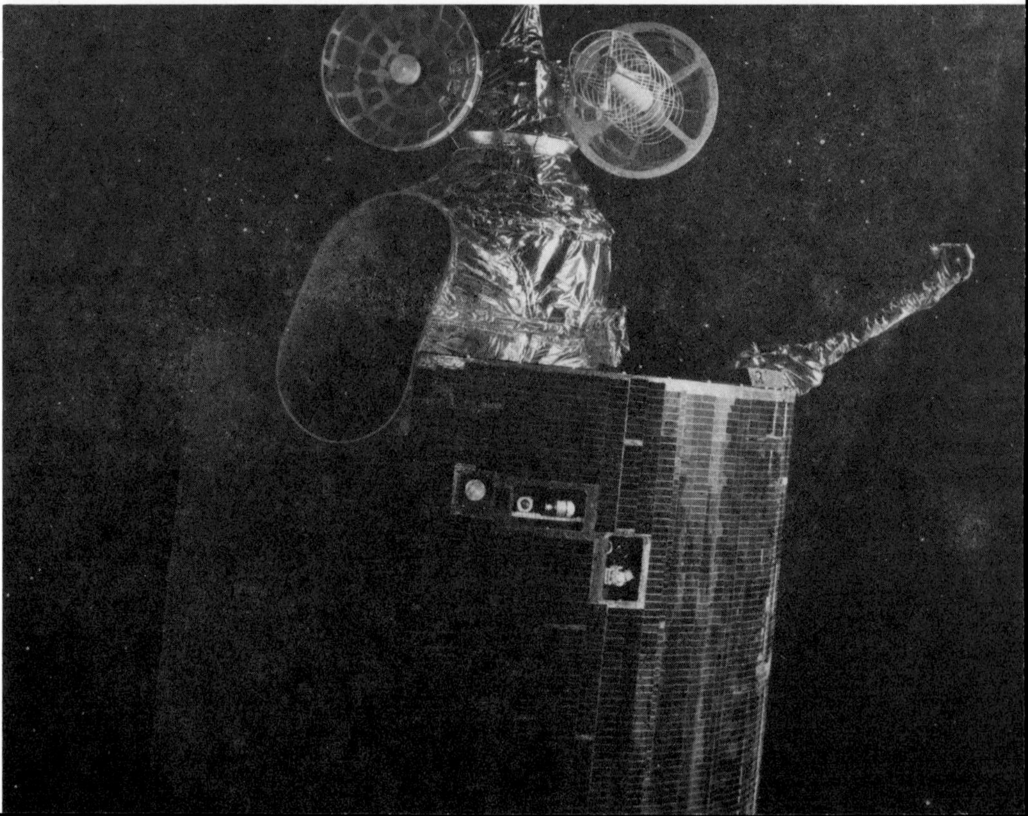

which *Landsat* satellites played the major role. Although they were originally launched by the United States, more than fifty countries throughout the world have profited from the information derived from these observation satellites.

Electromagnetic radiation coming from different areas and objects on the earth's surface is detected by multispectral scanners (MSS) aboard *Landsat* satellites orbiting more than 500 miles (800 km) above the earth. From information the satellites relay to ground stations, scientists can identify mineral and energy resources, detect pollution, analyze the composition of the soil, estimate crop production, construct accurate maps, discover areas that may face some natural disaster such as an earthquake, and help with other natural resource management programs.

As valuable as this information may be, remote-sensing satellites have raised many concerns and fears as well as legal problems. Obviously, satellites that can detect so much can also discover secret military installations. They can also detect industrial, transportation, and communications installations, which could be possible targets in the event of a war.

There is also the wider question of whether one country has the right to survey the land of another country and, if so, how the data collected should be used. Some have equated remote sensing with spying on another country. No one denies that some

Above: Tiros, *an early weather satellite;*
Below: *this* GOES *weather satellite was launched in the early 1980s.*

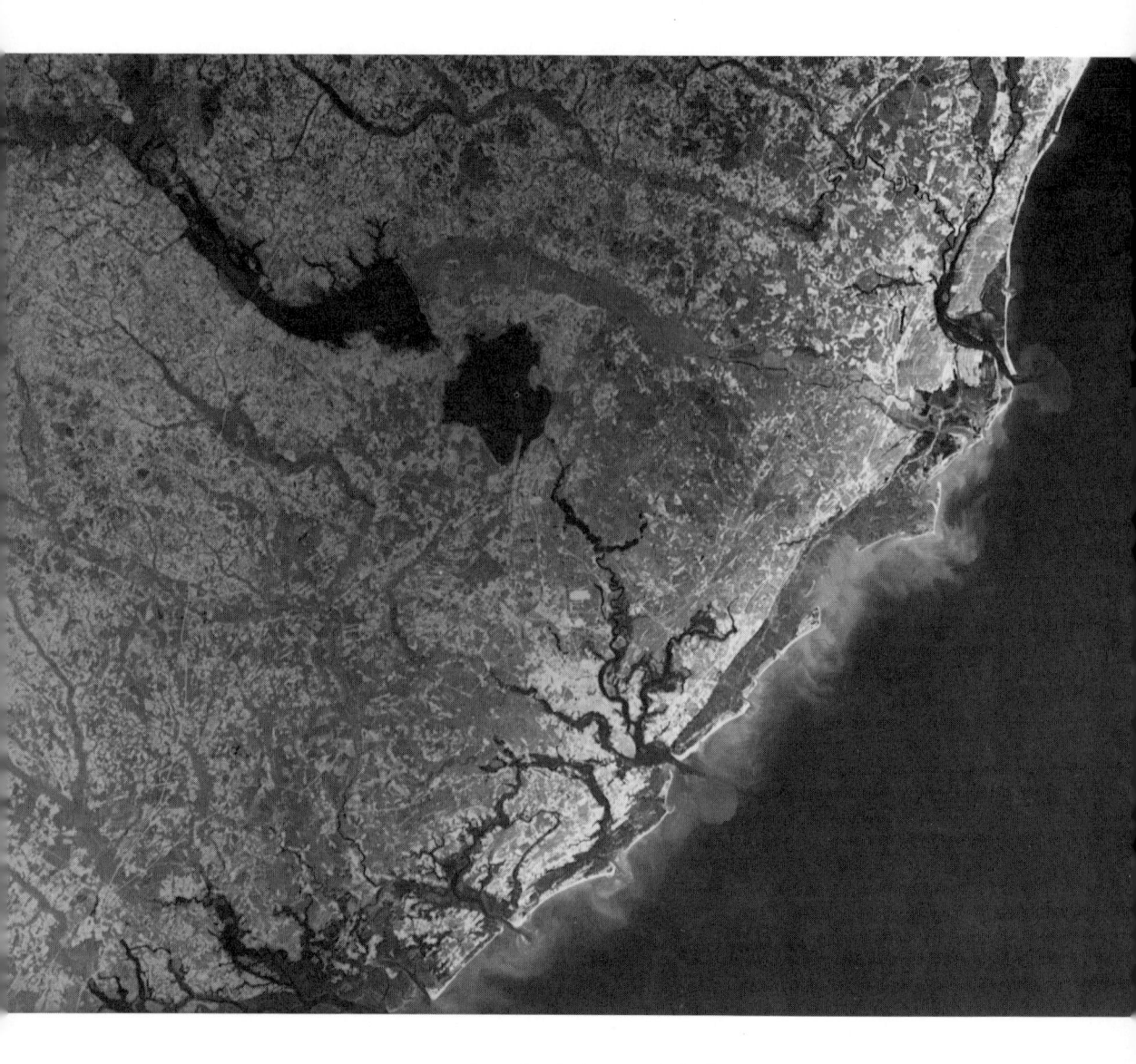

a Landsat 4 *coastal view*
of Charleston, South Carolina

satellites do indeed act as spies-in-the-sky for military and defense information. No matter what one thinks about spying upon other nations, the activity is as old as civilization itself. And there isn't any rule or principle of international law that prohibits the observation of another country from beyond that country's boundaries. Since outer space is considered beyond the territorial boundary of any nation, these satellites are technically operating within the law.

But what about peaceful uses of the data obtained from remote sensing? Does the United States, for example, have the right to collect data about Peru's natural resources without Peru's consent? Does the United States have the right to give that information to anyone it chooses, or only to Peru? Many less developed countries oppose the spreading of any remote-sensing information without their consent. They argue that the principle of state sovereignty, which is the keystone of international law, would be violated by such uncontrolled dissemination.

Some countries, such as the United States, believe that all countries should be free to conduct remote-sensing activities. The outer space treaties provide for the free use of space by all, and these observations are made outside of the observed country's territory. Also, the wide paths of the satellite's sensors cut across many national boundaries. It would be extremely difficult, if not impossible, to separate out data from each individual country. Out in space you can't see most national boundaries.

Actually, most nations are not as concerned about whether they are being observed as they are about the use of those observations. Latin American countries, for example, want the observed nation to have absolute control over any distribution of information about its resources, whether that be to another country, an international organization, or a private party. They argue that each nation has the exclusive right to that information as well as the right to dispose of that information as it chooses.

On the other hand, it is also clear that if remote sensing information can only be disseminated with the consent of the "sensed" country, there would eventually be information-rich and information-poor countries. Those countries with remote-sensing satellites would have all the information whereas those without sensing capability would have none.

There is no doubt that remote sensing can provide many benefits to humankind but, of course, it also can provide valuable information that could be exploited by another party both economically and militarily. Realistically, however, there is very little, if anything, that an observed nation can peacefully do to prevent its territory from being surveyed by satellites or prevent having the gathered information given to others. Therefore, in December 1986, the United Nations addressed this issue by adopting a resolution outlining a set of remote-sensing principles. These principles provide for the dissemination of remote-sensing information on a nondiscriminating basis, without requiring the consent of the sensed nation.

A similar problem in reverse arose from direct broadcast satellites (DBS). Instead of requiring an extensive network of ground stations to relay transmissions to home receivers, as the communications satellites currently in operation do, DBS is able to beam signals directly into individual homes or any other buildings equipped with the appropriate receivers.

Although there is very little, if any, commercial DBS service yet, experimental programs have shown that these systems are not only possible but actually give much better reception than the current communications satellites. Not only will more channels be available, but also DBS technology will provide television service to remote regions on earth that currently have none. And countries that do not have enough qualified teachers or have an inadequate network of ground stations can use DBS to upgrade their educational systems.

Direct broadcast satellites sound like something everyone should favor, but that is not the case. Many nations fear that DBS will be used by neighboring countries to broadcast propaganda or programs that are politically offensive. There will be no way for any government to stop these broadcasts from being received by its citizens because they are direct and bypass any retransmission stations. Even if a broadcast is intended only for the citizens of a specific country, the surface pattern, or "footprint," of the satellite cannot always be shaped to the contours of that country's territory, and spillover, although unintentional, is unavoidable.

Since 1968 a UN committee had been trying to draft a set of principles on the use of DBS, but it was unable to reach agreements on key issues. One of these was whether prior consent of the receiving state was necessary before DBS signals could be beamed into a country. The United States and most of the industrialized Western countries favored the concept of free flow of information without the consent of any governmental agency, whereas the Soviet Union and many of the developing countries wanted much more regulation, specifically the expressed consent of the receiving state.

In other words, although the disagreement between the United States and the Soviet Union was based upon the fundamental differences between the ideologies of the two countries, neither country was alone in its stand on this issue. However, a majority of states supported the prior consent rule and argued that it was the right of a sovereign state to protect itself from unwanted transmissions, even if it curtailed the rights of individual human beings. This majority opinion prevailed, and in 1982, the United Nations adopted by vote a General Assembly resolution requiring the consent of the receiving state before broadcasts can be sent into its country.

Thus, although the question of where outer space begins has never been resolved, some progress has been made in reaching a consensus about the uses of outer space. Undoubtedly, there will be many other controversies similar to these in the future, just as there will be some about matters pertaining to the uses of terrestrial regions. But perhaps the greatest threats to the peaceful use of outer space are the enormous advances that have taken place in the field of space weaponry. We must now look at that aspect of outer space.

CHAPTER SIX

STAR WARS AND THE LAW

It is no secret that both the United States and the Soviet Union are engaged in intensive research and development of space weaponry. Although all of the outer space treaties state that outer space is to be used for peaceful purposes only, the term "peaceful" has generally been interpreted as meaning "nonaggressive," not necessarily nonmilitary. By international agreements, nuclear weapons and weapons of mass destruction have been banned from earth orbit, outer space, or the surface of the moon and other celestial bodies. But the treaties do not ban weapons meant for defensive purposes, only offensive ones. Many critics have pointed out, however, that it is not always possible to classify a weapon as purely defensive or purely offensive.

The outer space treaties also ban the testing of weapons on the moon or other celestial bodies but do not prohibit such tests in earth orbit or in outer space. This is agreeable to the military establishments because outer space is viewed as a much more valuable resource for military exploitation than the moon. Outer

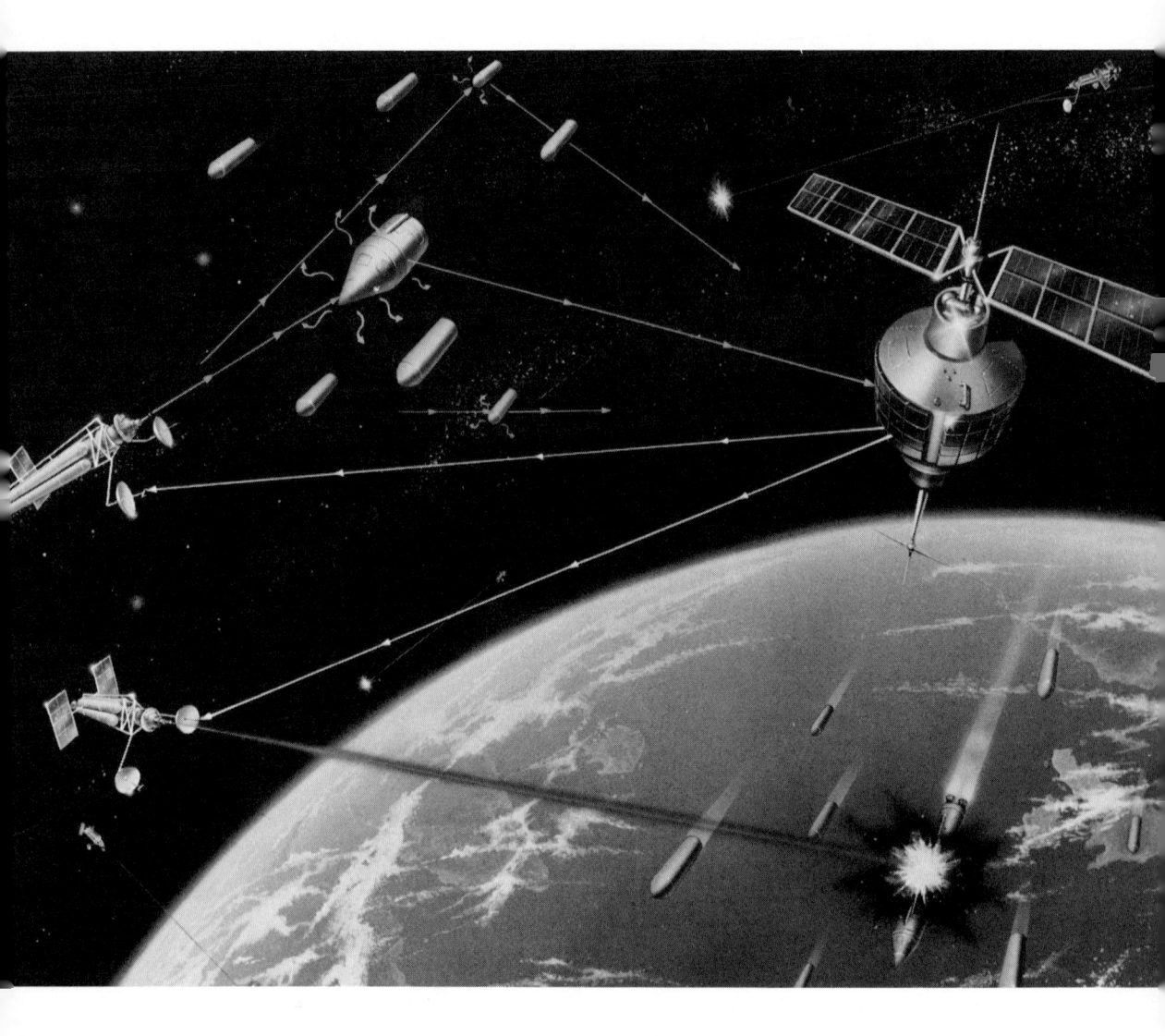

*one artist's conception of what
a war in space would look like*

space completely surrounds the earth, and, therefore, it provides access to any point on the globe. It is a natural military staging area for either offensive or defensive purposes. It also provides an excellent means of surveillance because the high altitudes that satellites can reach give them very wide line-of-sight vistas. This surveillance ability has led to new and sophisticated procedures for detecting hostile military buildups or maneuvers. It also increases the ability to quickly relay military communications.

The treaties thus do not explicitly ban conflicts in space, nor the use of space to aid in terrestrial conflicts. Manned or unmanned military orbiting spacecraft are allowed, as are military personnel on nonmilitary craft. In fact, most of the astronauts and cosmonauts have been drawn from the military of their respective countries. It is no wonder, therefore, that recent advances in space technology and the continuing escalation of the arms race in both the United States and the Soviet Union have raised great concern about whether the military use of space can be controlled.

Examples of space-oriented weaponry include antisatellite weapon systems (ASATs) and antiballistic missiles. These weapons are based on laser or particle-beam technology. With the increase of research into these weaponry fields, a few new names, including the Strategic Defense Initiative (SDI) and "Star Wars," have become the commonly used terms when referring to these outer space defense systems. As has been noted, however, there is very little difference between weapons designed to defend one's territory and weapons designed to attack someone else's land. In most cases they are the same equipment, although supposedly designated for different purposes. It is not surprising, therefore, that what one country terms a defensive weapon another may view as offensive, especially if the weapon is aimed directly at its territory.

Can international law control or discourage military conflict in space? Let us look at some possible examples of military conflicts that might arise in outer space.

Obviously, a physical attack by whatever means on a manned or unmanned space object would clearly be an act of aggression. It certainly would call for a strong protest and a demand for compensation. It might also prompt a military response or some other retaliatory course of action. To avoid escalating the conflict, however, the attacked country might appeal to some international legal body as a first step in such a situation. This would be most likely if the attack was not viewed as a declaration of war.

But instead of making an outright attack on a spacecraft, suppose someone or some country places nuclear weapons in space or on the moon. This, of course, would create a definite threat to others and would openly violate the outer space treaties. Such an offense would have to be confirmed first, and even at that early stage many problems arise.

Two space-based weapons currently being explored for their possible development. Above is a hyper-velocity railgun, a type of kinetic energy weapon. Below is a homing-and-kill device used to track and intercept ICBM reentry vehicles.

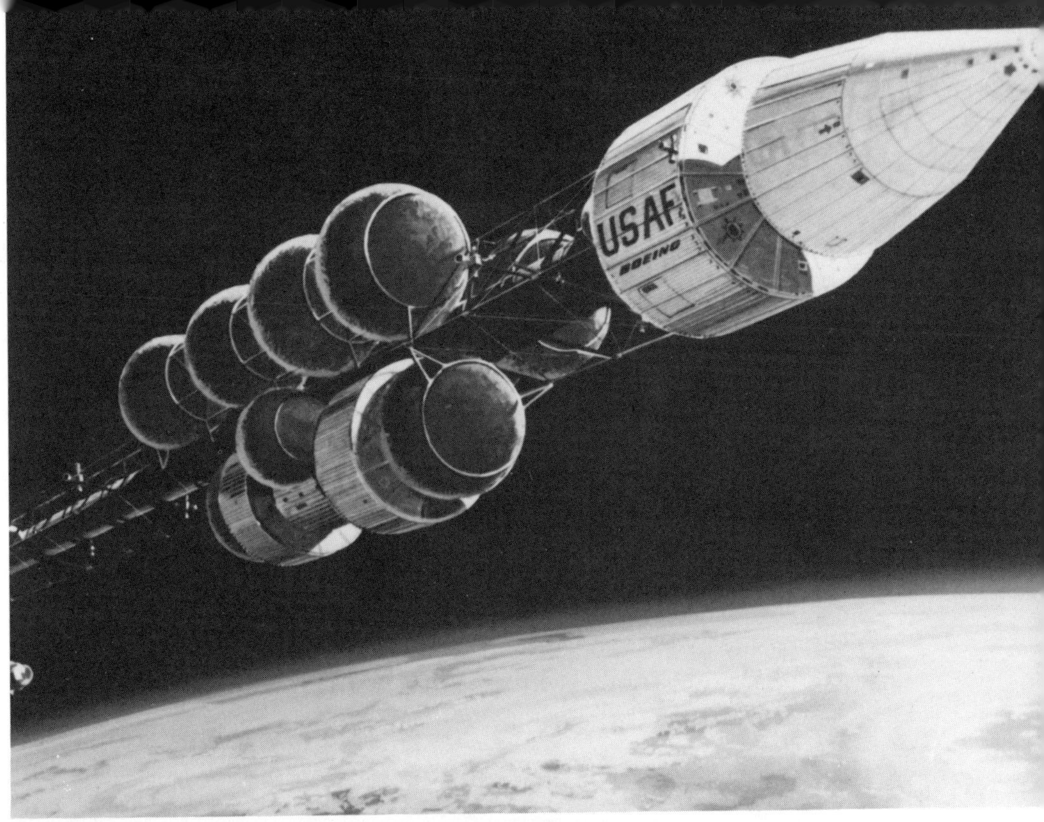
USAF
BOEING

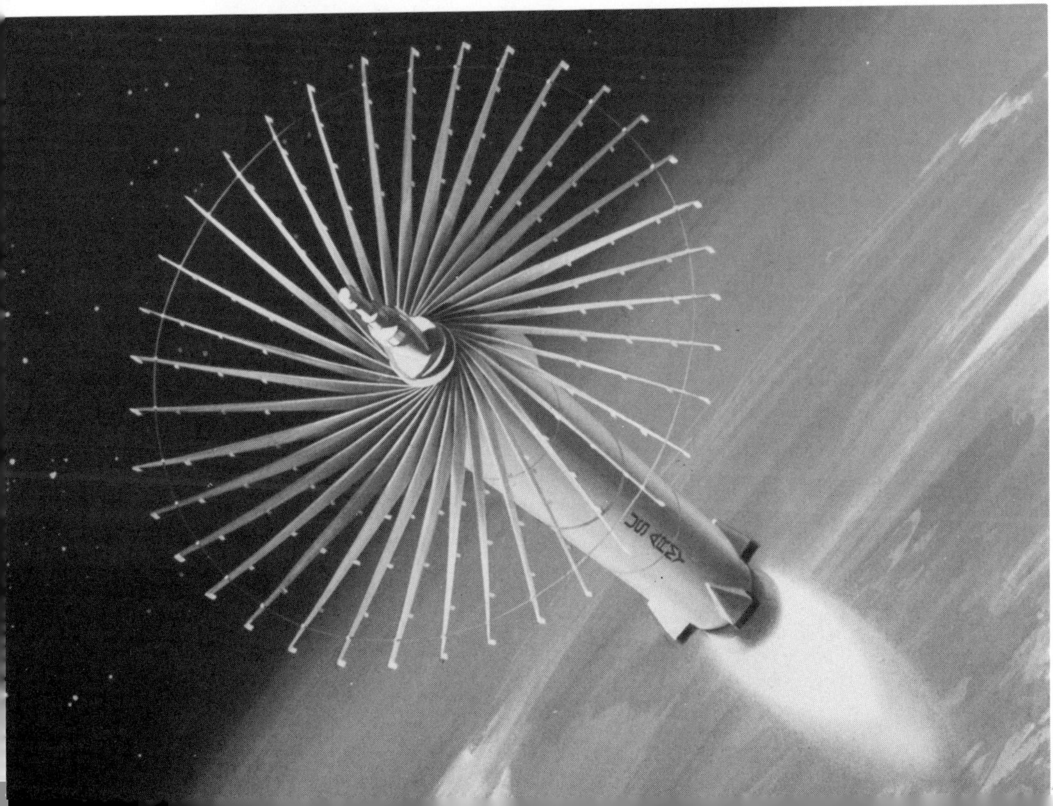

As you may have noted, none of the treaties provides for mandatory on-site inspections of an orbiting spacecraft. No one can board a spacecraft without the permission of the country that owns it. To do so would be a violation of national sovereignty and against international law. And even if proof were somehow obtained of the existence of forbidden weaponry, no sanctions are provided against any nation for such violations. These omissions were caused by the inability of the major treaty signers to agree upon such provisions.

Although the treaties do provide mandatory inspections of lunar bases, this is only permissible on a reciprocal basis. In other words, you can look at my base if I can look at yours. Of course, any country with a military installation on the moon would be very reluctant to enter into such an agreement. None has shown much openness about weaponry here on earth, and it is doubtful that in outer space we would behave any differently.

It is possible, therefore, that at some point a "zone of security" around a space station or a lunar base might be instituted. This would prevent outsiders from entering the area and would, in effect, establish a declaration of sovereignty over the region. Not only would this violate treaty provisions, but it might also interfere with another nation's exploration or utilization of space. This would be especially true if many such "zones of security" were created.

In this picture, an earth-generated laser beam is being reflected toward a target in space by a space-based mirror.

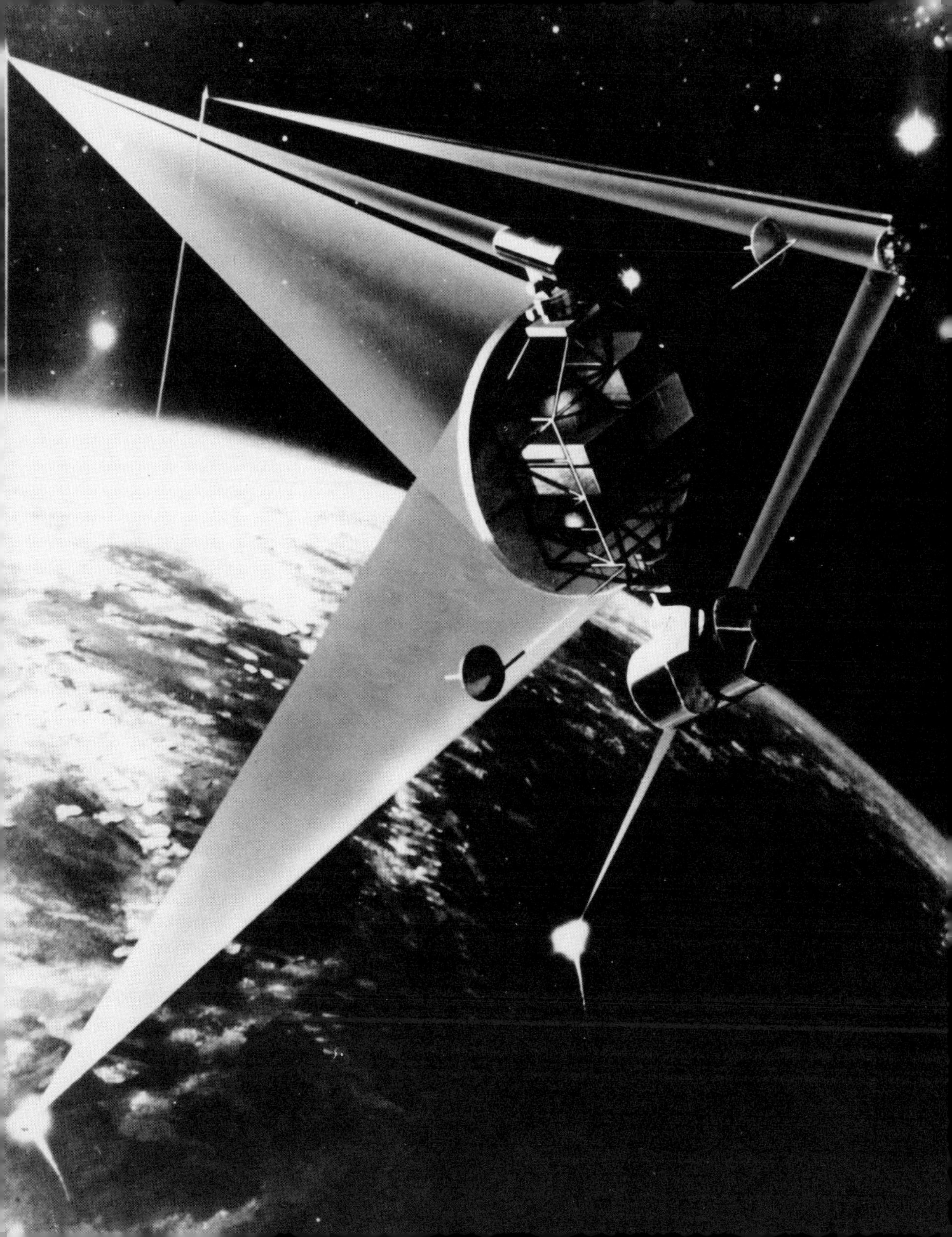

Thus, the military presence in space has and will continue to create a host of legal issues, questions, and problems. The military use of space must somehow be legally restricted either solely to defensive purposes or banned entirely from this region. The international space law community must provide a strong legal framework that allows space industrialization to grow safely with internationally agreed-upon rights and obligations.

To a large extent, however, the degree to which the two major powers pursue militarization of space depends upon how safe each feels with whatever defensive land-based weapons it has available, and what progress has been made toward mutual disarmament, both on earth and in space. At this time each side clearly fears the other will gain an advantage and, therefore, is ready to increase its strategic and tactical strength, even though such efforts give no guarantee of real security.

At some point, one would hope, a more sensible viewpoint will prevail, and perhaps then efforts can be directed toward an agreement on an international treaty that effectively prevents the militarization of space. This would include, of course, the necessary inspection procedures to ensure verification of the agreement.

Whether or not such agreements are possible, there is no doubt that our technological advances will soon enable us to have a permanent manned presence in space. Then space law will have to not only consider the problems raised by weapons in space but also the legal rights of permanent space residents. To what extent will they be permitted to control their own affairs and make their own laws? The problems and questions that will arise are of a different nature than those we have been talking about. We must now turn our attention to this subject.

CHAPTER SEVEN

SPACE COLONY LAW

The year is A.D. 2200. A new group of pioneers has just arrived at the Galileo Base camp on the moon. They are ready to begin their three-week orientation sessions before being transported to their final destination—Space Colony I. It is there that these modern-day settlers hope to make their permanent homes.

Space Colony I is already a thriving community. Babies have been born there, and schools have been established. Plans for a colony university are under way, although at present college-age students must return to earth for their advanced studies. Most of them, however, plan to return to SC, as it is called by its inhabitants, because it offers far more opportunities than can be found back on earth. Engineers, scientists, and manufacturers are in the greatest demand, but now that the colony has grown so large, there are also positions available in education, government, sales, newspapers and television, sanitation, restaurants, and many other fields.

For the last twenty-five or thirty years, more and more people have been moving up to Space Colony I, and the waiting list is

*one artist's concept of a
twenty-first century space colony*

already quite long. There are many who want to get away from the overcrowded earth to start a new life in space. In fact, the flow of population is now becoming so great that construction of another space colony has already been started. It will also be placed in orbit around the earth and will be roomy enough for at least 25,000 people, just like Space Colony I.

Although SC I has a local government similar to that of a small city, it is still considered a possession of the United States and must adhere to that country's laws and regulations. Its inhabitants are either U.S. citizens or have special permits from the United States to be there. All industry and manufacturing is subject to the same regulations, controls, and taxes as their earthbound counterparts.

One problem that has already arisen is the competition that these industries in space are creating with manufacturers on earth. The factories in space can use the weightlessness and near-vacuum conditions of outer space to make certain products that are both superior and cheaper than those produced on earth. Some earthbound industries see this production as an economic threat and are calling for stricter controls of the space-made products. They want tariffs put on the space products so that they cannot be sold so cheaply. It is unfair competition, they claim, especially since these space industries were originally given their impetus by the U.S. government, which not only helped establish them but also gave them many tax breaks in their early years of development.

But there are other earthbound industries that welcome the products made in space. Since we are looking way into the future, we don't know exactly what these products may be, but if the past is any example, we know they will be worth the effort.

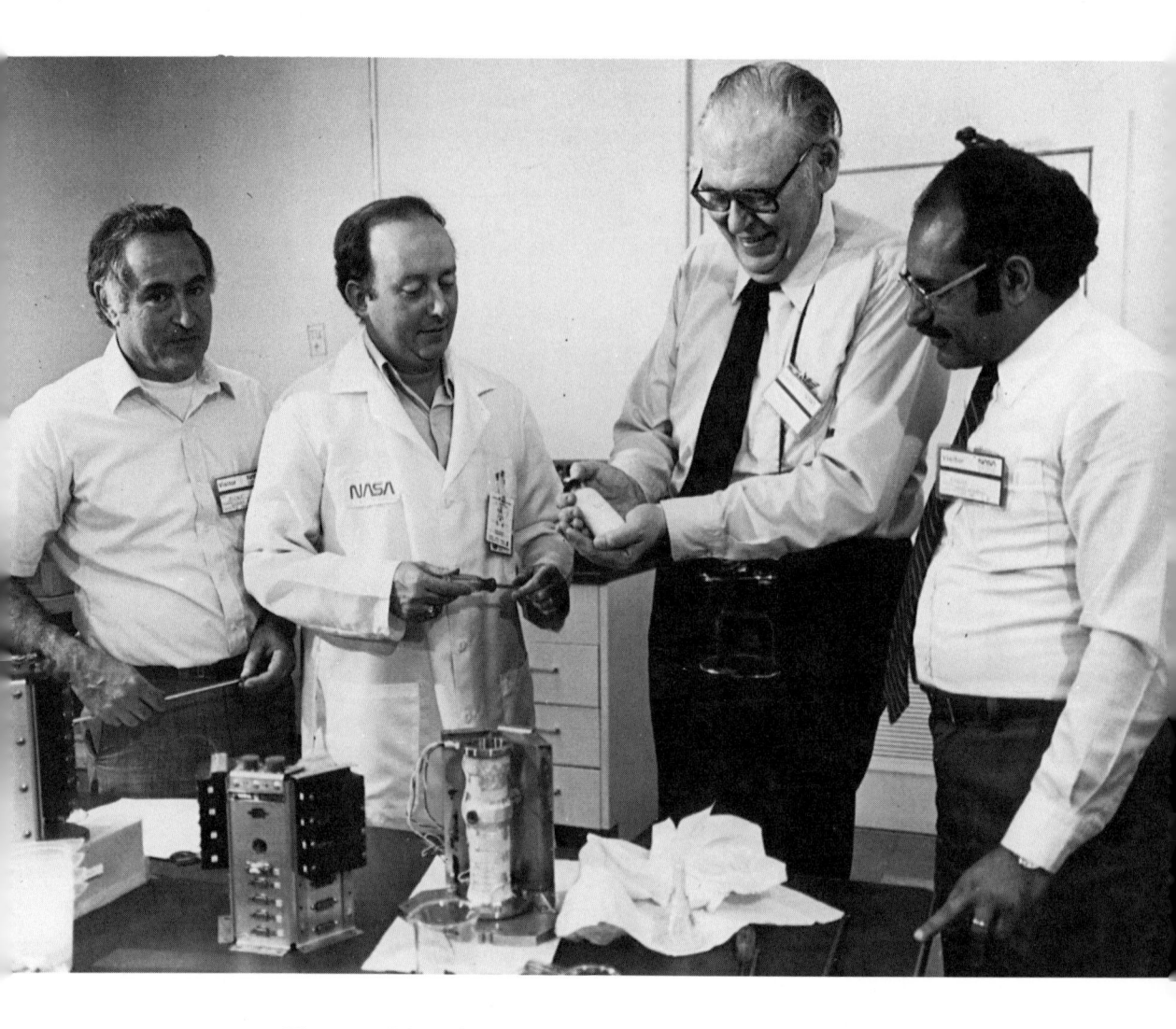

The small latex beads being held here were produced during a manufacturing experiment aboard a space shuttle flight. They should prove useful in the calibration of medical and scientific instruments.

For example, during the space shuttle *Challenger*'s mission in February 1984, almost perfectly formed tiny plastic beads were manufactured in the weightless environment of space. No process here on earth could have produced as perfect a sphere as that accomplished in space. These polystyrene beads, each only $3/100$ths of a millimeter in diameter, are being used in laboratories and factories to calibrate measuring devices and to regulate the dosages of certain medicines and amounts of other chemicals.

The polystyrene beads are but one example of the kinds of space products that will benefit all of us. Industrial applications of space technology already have been used in the cars we drive, the tools we use, the pots and pans we cook in, and the clothes we wear. All sorts of Space-Age devices are being used in the medical field to help diagnose illnesses, monitor patients, aid in surgical procedures, and assist the handicapped. When many more experiments are conducted in the environment of outer space, as will be possible in a space colony, medical science will benefit even more people. It is even thought that perhaps someday people with weak hearts or other debilitating diseases will find it much easier to live in a space colony. Areas in the colony in which there is less gravitational pull, and therefore less stress on the heart, may be set aside for such patients.

Of course, the United States is not the only country that is planning to put a colony into space. In all likelihood, by the time SC I is in operation, the Soviet Union will also have placed its own colony in earth orbit. It will be operated by the Soviet government just as SC I will be under U.S. control. However, it will probably be under stricter military supervision than SC I, and only selected personnel will be allowed to colonize it. Its industries will also manufacture space products, but, for the most part, these will be used solely by the Soviets and their allies. There is, however, always the possibility that the Soviets may choose to sell excess products on the world market, creating another possible economic problem for manufacturers.

Will this be the scene in outer space one or two hundred years from now? If so, what will it be like in, say, five hundred years? By then there will be many more colonies established and thriving. Or perhaps several will have been linked together to create large regions, possibly approaching the size of a small nation on earth.

Areas for growing crops, raising livestock, operating factories, and engaging in other business enterprises will be purposely built into the original colony designs so that they will be largely self-sufficient. They will be able to trade successfully with those on earth as well as with other colonies in space.

And, as they become more independent and larger, they will undoubtedly want a greater voice in the running of their government. They may even be able to separate themselves from their mother country and establish an independent nation—a republic of space. This may be similar to the separation of the American colonies from England two hundred years ago. However, it is to be hoped that a revolutionary war will not be necessary to accomplish this. It could destroy the space colony itself.

What kind of government will be chosen by the new republic of space? From historical example, we know that when people are free to choose their own system of government, their choice largely reflects the inhabitants' previous experiences with governments. Those who grew up in a democracy will probably opt for a similar kind of government. However, because of the many perils of living in space, more control over certain individual and

This space colony could hold 10,000 people in its earthlike environment inside a vast wheel more than a mile (1.6 km) in diameter.

group activities may have to be imposed than might be necessary on earth.

For example, someone or some group must have complete authority to oversee and regulate the daily operations of the colony. The air quality must be kept stable; the water supply must be monitored and adjusted if necessary; the slow rotation of the entire space colony that produces the effects of a false gravity must be kept accurate. And anyone who is a threat to the operation of the colony must be apprehended and forced to leave. Unless the colony is enormous, it is doubtful that long-term prisoners will be tolerated. Space will be too precious to waste on a large prison facility.

Any colonies owned by the Soviet Union, if they should be able to free themselves from that country's control, will probably attempt a mixture of democratic and socialistic government. Privately owned enterprises will not exist at first, and the government will still control much of the colony's operation and production. It is possible that over time, because all the space colonies face the same problems of survival in space, their forms of government will become quite similar, regardless of their histories. Private businesses will be allowed to grow but only under the strict controls of a government that is dedicated to preserving the health and safety of the space colony and its citizens.

If we look beyond the establishment of space colonies, the next step is to send manned spacecraft out beyond the solar system, to the stars. These will eventually explore and perhaps colonize the rest of the galaxy. To do this will require crews willing to spend many years, if not the rest of their lives, away from the earth. It will require people who know that they will never reach another solar system in their lifetimes but are willing to leave that privilege to their children, grandchildren, or even great grandchildren, who will be born during the journey.

Although a system of government can be set up initially for such a spacecraft, once it has left our solar system and is headed for the stars, the legal institutions that were left back on the earth will have absolutely no control over the daily activities aboard the craft. The captain of the spacecraft, like the captain of a ship on the ocean, will assume command at the beginning of the journey. But it is impossible to predict how long or how effective that control will be. Illnesses, disagreements, or even mutinies can change the best-laid plans. Science fiction writers have used such scenarios as the basis for many of their stories.

And since the spacecraft may never return to earth, those left behind may never know its fate. But wherever it goes and for however long it takes to get there, one fact will be true. Some form of law, some set of rules, will be in effect aboard that craft. The laws and the ruling group may change either peacefully or violently over time, but once some order is reestablished, it will have to be accompanied by some form of legal system. Laws or rules of behavior exist wherever humankind is found.

SOURCES USED

When the research for this book was being done, the major information about space law was to be found in the many law-review journals. Hardly anything on space law appeared in the many books dealing with space exploration. Those few that did mention the subject devoted at most only two or three paragraphs to it. Although much more has since been written about space law, it is still a topic found mainly in the law review journals and magazines devoted to space exploration. The following list includes some of the sources used in researching *Space Law*.

Altman, Robert. "The Food and Drug Administration: Regulation of Production in Space." *Food, Drug, Cosmetic Law Journal*, 1984, no. 39, pp. 445–461.

Brumberg, Bruce. "Regulating Private Space Transportation." *Administrative Law Review*, no. 36, 1984, pp. 363–385.

Cheng, Bin. "The Legal Status of Outer Space and Relevant Issues: Delimitation of Outer Space and Definition of Peaceful Use." *Journal of Space Law,* vol. 11, spring/fall 1983, pp. 89–105.

Christol, Carl Q. "The Common Interest in the Exploration, Use and Exploitation of Outer Space for Peaceful Purposes: The Soviet-American Dilemma." *Akron Law Review* (fall 1984), pp. 193–222.

Deem, Charles, L. "Liability of Private Space Transportation Companies to Their Customers." *Insurance Counsel Journal*, July 1984, pp. 340–361.

Dula, Art. "Private Sector Activities in Outer Space." *The International Lawyer,* winter 1985, vol. 19, no. 1, pp. 159–187.

Gorove, Stephen. "Law and Security in Outer Space: Current Issues of Space Law Before the United Nations." *Journal of Space Law,* spring/fall 1983, pp. 5–13.

Haggerty, James J. "The Outlook for Space Commercialization." *Space World,* May 1985, pp. 20–25.

Meredith, Pamela L. "The Legality of a High-Technology Missile Defense System: The ABM and Outer Space Treaties." *The American Journal of International Law,* April 1984, vol. 78, pp. 418–423.

Merter, Martin. "Peaceful Uses of Outer Space and National Security." *The International Lawyer,* summer 1983, vol. 17, no. 3, pp. 581–596.

Reichhardt, Tony. "Toward an International Solar System." *Space World,* April 1985, pp. 24–26.

Schnapf, Lawrence. "Explorations in Space Law: An Examination of the Legal Issues Raised by Geostationary, Remote Sensing and Direct Broadcasting Satellites." *New York Law School Law Review,* 1985, vol. 29, no. 4, pp. 687–748.

Smith, Delbert D.; Lopatkiewicz, Stefan M.; and Rothblatt, Martin A. "Legal Implications of a Permanent Manned Presence in Space." *West Virginia Law Review,* summer 1983, vol. 85, no. 5, pp. 857–872.

Wagner, Rice Sumner. "The Lawmen Head for Space." *Space World,* May 1984, pp. 8–9.

Wassenbergh, H. A. "The Unfreedom Under Outer Space Law." *Air Law,* vol. X, no. 3, 1985, pp. 161–172.

INDEX

Airspace, 13, 14, 17, 26, 58
American flag on moon, 49
    and *Apollo* 15, 50
Andromeda Galaxy, 23
Antiballistic missiles, 73
Apogee, satellite high point, 60
Apollo 15, 50
    moon mission, 28, 29
ASATs and missiles, 73
Aussat, satellite, 54

Balloons, 61–62
Baseball and rules, 34
Boeing Company, 41
Bogota Declaration, 56–57

Canada, *Cosmos 954* and, 26

Celestial Bodies,
    agreement on, 43
    and the moon, 39–40, 43–44, 47
    and nuclear weapons, 71
    resources of, 48
    and treaties, 39–40, 43–44, 50
    weightlessness on, 45
Challenger, space shuttle, 27
    beads, 82, 83
Charter, United Nations, 37, 38; See also United Nations
Chernobyl nuclear accident, 26
Chinese and gunpower, 9
Communication satellites, 54
    and DBS, 68, 68–69

— 91 —

Communication satellites *(continued)*
    geostationary orbit of, 53
    Indonesian, 31
    orbital position of, 56
    and outer space, 57
    and rockets, 32

Delta rocket, 11
Direct and broadcast satellites (DBS), 68
    and ground stations, 69

Echo, satellite, 54
Electromagnetic radiation, 63
    and MSS, 65
English common-law, 37

FCC, 56

Galileo Base Camp, 79
Gamma rays, 63
Gemini space program, 63
Geostationary orbit, 11, 50
    and ITU, 56
    and outer space, 58
    and satellites, 53, 55
    and territories, 57

Geostationary satellite, 53
Goes, satellite, 64
Ground stations, 53, 63
    and DBS, 68–69
    and satellites, 65

ICBM reentry vehicle, 75
Industrial technology, 83
Insurance Companies, 32
    and liability, 42
International agency, 44, 56
International conventions, 42
    agreements of, 48, 60
    and territory, 14
International law, 14, 32, 37
    and airspace, 58, 67
    and military conflict, 74
    and military presence, 78
    and orbiting spacecraft, 76
    and space treaties, 39, 42
    and United Nations, 47
International treaties, 26, 44
International Telecommunication Union (ITU), 56
    and United States, 57

Kinetic energy weapon, 75

Landsat 4, 66
    satellites, 65
Laser beam, 77
    particle technology, 73
Law(s),
    are formalized rules, 33
    aviation, 13
    common, 13, 37
    and Constitution, 37
    international, 14, 32, 37
    orbiting spacecraft, 76
    in outer space, 17, 47
    space, 13, 42, 47, 78
    and space stations, 29
    and treaties, 57
    zoning, 35
Liability Convention, 42
Lindbergh, Charles, 14
Lunar
    bases, 76
    mining operation, 28
    resources, 44, 48

Medical science and space, 83
Mercury space program, 63
Milky Way, 18, 21
Moon, 19, 39–40, 45, 47, 50
    and Galileo Base, 79

Moon *(continued)*
    materials, 29, 43, 44
    and nuclear weapons, 71
    and satellites, 53
    and treaties, 74, 76
Moon Treaty, 43, 48
Multinational space crews, 29
Multispectral scanner (MSS), 65

NASA
    launch facilities, 42
    and space colonies, 50
North Star, 21
Nuclear
    reactor, 26
    weapons, 71, 74

Orbital maneuvering vehicle, 41
Orbiting space station, 41
Outer space, 13, 17, 22, 58
    boundaries, 60, 67
    business enterprises, 84
    colony, 83
    conflict, 37, 57, 73–74
    defense systems, 73
    and laws, 32

Outer space *(continued)*
    and lawyers, 61
    legal meaning of, 48
    -made products, 81, 83
    and the moon, 74, 76
    objects, 42, 43
    risks of, 45
    and satellites, 57
    and space shuttles, 29
    surveillance, 73
    treaties, 26, 39–40, 50
    and weaponry, 70, 71
Outer Space Treaty 1967, 39–40
    and the Moon Treaty, 43
    and national boundaries, 67
    and weaponry, 71

Perigee, satellite close point, 60, 61
Pioneer 10, satellite, 22
Pioneer spacecraft, 24
Planet(s), 18, 29
    Mars, 39
    Pluto, 21

Registration Convention, 43

Remote sensing
    and electromagnetic radiation, 63
    information, 67, 68
    satellites, 61, 65
    and the Space Age, 61
    weather forecasting, 62
Return and Rescue Agreement, 40
Rockwell International, 51

Salyut, space station, 29
Satellite(s), 55
    communication, 31, 53–54
    footprint, 69
    in orbit, 53, 57, 60
    orbital positions, 56
    remote-sensing, 61, 65
    Russian *Cosmos 954*, 26
    sky spies, 37, 39, 67
    Sputnik 1, 9
    surveying, 68, 73
    weather, 11, 63, 64
SDI weaponry field, 73
Sirius (Dog Star), 21
Skylab space station, 30, 46
    American, 29
Solar radiation, 45
Solar system, 21, 22

Soviet Union, 9, 26, 39, 84, 86
    and DBS signals, 69
    and Moon Treaty, 43
    and space colonies, 83
    space weaponry, 71, 73
    and United States, 47, 50
Space Age, 9, 22, 37
    devices, 83
    and remote sensing, 61
Space-based weapons, 70, 71, 75
Space colony, 50, 80, 81, 85
    and false gravity, 86
    and gravitational pull, 83
    independance, 84
Space Colony 1 (SC1), 79, 81, 83
Spacecraft, 9, 20, 21, 26, 61
    and experiments, 32
    and gravity, 45
    military orbiting, 73
    on celestial bodies, 50
    orbital path of, 43
    orbiting, 76
    personnel, 40, 42
    and solar system, 86–87
    and space junk, 39
    and space lawyers, 58
    and treaties, 74

Space law, 13, 42, 47
Space laywers, 32, 50, 58
Space oriented weaponry, 73
Spaceship Earth, 18
Space shuttle, 27, 29, 61, 83
Space station, 39, 51
Space technology, 47, 73, 83
Spatial (boundary), 60
Sputnik, 9, 10
Star Wars, 73

Telstar, satellite, 54
Thruster jets, 53, 55
Tiros, satellite, 64

United Nations, 43, 47, 48
    agency (ITU), 56
    Charter, 37, 38
    and DBS, 69, 70
    and outer space, 60
    and remote sensing, 68
United States, 9, 22, 39, 65
    agreements, 40, 42–43
    and *Apollo* mission, 29
    Constitution, 37
    and Cuba, 14
    and DBS signals, 69
    and FCC, 56
    government, 32

United States *(continued)*
    laws and regulations, 81
    and Moon Treaty, 43
    and orbit regions, 55
    and Peru, 67
    and Soviet Union, 47, 50
    and space colonies, 83
    and space programs, 63
    space weaponry, 71, 73

Viking spacecraft, 20
Voyager 1, satellite, 22

Voyager 2 spacecraft, 20, 25

Weapon(s)
    kinetic energy, 75
    mass-destruction, 43
    nuclear, 40
Weather satellite, 11, 63
Weightlessness, 45

X rays, 63

Zones of security, 76